YESTERDAY, TODAY, AND FOREVER

YESTERDAY, TODAY, AND FOREVER

M. RUSSELL BALLARD

TIMELESS GOSPEL MESSAGES

With insights from his grandfathers
MELVIN J. BALLARD *and* HYRUM MACK SMITH

DESERET BOOK

SALT LAKE CITY, UTAH

For the descendants of
Grandfather Hyrum Mack Smith
and Grandfather Melvin J. Ballard

Images on pages viii and ix courtesy Intellectual Reserve, Inc. Used by permission.

Visit us at DeseretBook.com

Library of Congress Cataloging-in-Publication Data

(CIP on file)
ISBN 978-1-62972-042-5

Printed in the United States of America
Publishers Printing, Salt Lake City, UT

10 9 8 7 6 5 4 3 2 1

Contents

Preface

I love the gospel of Jesus Christ. It is a great joy to me to be able to stand as a witness of our Savior and Redeemer and to teach in many settings the principles that will lead us to eternal life. This collection of messages was gathered from talks I have given over the thirty-eight years of my service as a General Authority. They were given in a variety of settings and places other than general conference. They are being published here for the first time along with doctrinal statements of my grandfathers.

It is a humbling reality and a great joy of my life to claim as my grandfathers two Apostles of the Lord Jesus Christ: My mother's father, Elder Hyrum Mack Smith, who served in the Quorum of the Twelve from 1901 to 1918, and my father's father, Elder Melvin J. Ballard, who served from 1919 to 1939. Both men accomplished a great work in their apostolic ministries, touching the lives of many individual people they met. Additionally, their teachings blessed the lives of a generation of Latter-day Saints who heard them speak in person, and more than two generations who have read their printed sermons and teachings.

My grandfather Hyrum Mack Smith was born in 1872 to Joseph F. and Edna Lambson Smith. Joseph F. gave my grandfather the name Hyrum to honor his father, Hyrum Smith (1800–1844), and the name Mack to honor his grandmother Lucy Mack Smith (1775–1856). Hyrum Mack was raised in a household of faith by parents who were dedicated and devoted to each other and to

Hyrum Mack Smith

the restored gospel. His father was an Apostle who later became President of the Church.

My grandfather married my grandmother Ida Bowman in November 1895 and departed for his first mission in the British Isles shortly thereafter, laboring in England until 1898. He was twenty-nine years old when he was called to the apostleship in 1901, the first Apostle called in the twentieth century. Hyrum Mack presided over the Church's mission in Europe during the difficult period just before and following the outbreak of World War I, between 1913 and 1916. My mother was nine when they left for Europe, and from her I learned about Hyrum and his ministry.

During Hyrum Mack's ministry, he co-wrote in 1916 the widely influential *Doctrine and Covenants Commentary*. Two years later, in 1918, he died at the relatively young age of forty-five years. At his death, an article in the Church's monthly magazine stated, "On earth he was a teacher of righteousness, an advocate of justice, and an exemplar of purity. In the world to come, glory, immortality and eternal life are his" ("Hyrum Mack Smith," 377).

My grandfather Melvin J. Ballard was born in 1875 to Henry and Margaret McNeal Ballard. His parents were among the first settlers in Logan, Utah, and his father was the Logan Second Ward bishop, a calling he held for nearly forty years.

My grandfather married my grandmother Martha A. Jones in June 1896 and departed for his first mission shortly thereafter, serving in the Northern States Mission until 1898. My father, Melvin Russell Ballard Sr., was born while he labored in this mission.

MELVIN J. BALLARD

After a second but short mission to Idaho, Melvin was set apart as president of the Northwestern States Mission in 1909. He served tirelessly in that assignment until he was released in 1919, at which time he was called to the Quorum of the Twelve Apostles.

During his ministry, Melvin dedicated South America for the preaching of the gospel and prophesied of the remarkable growth we have witnessed in that great land. He also shared with the Church an awe-inspiring dream of the resurrected Savior; that vision was the foundation of his personal witness of Jesus Christ.

I was born in 1928, nearly eleven years before my Grandfather Ballard died in 1939. Since we lived in Salt Lake City, I got to know him as a grandson.

He was sixty-six years old when he died. My father, who was sitting at his bedside, told me that Grandfather pushed himself up in bed, looked around his hospital room as though he were addressing a congregation or a group, and said clearly, "And above all else, brethren, let us think straight." I don't go into my office any day of the week that I don't see those printed words displayed on the wall.

In studying the sermons and service of these two great and dedicated servants of the Lord, I was reminded of the truth that "God is the same yesterday, today, and forever" (Mormon 9:9; see also Doctrine and Covenants 20:12; 1 Nephi 10:18). Programs and even policies may change, circumstances in the world change, especially as we draw closer to the Second Coming of the Lord, but the doctrine of the gospel is eternal in nature, and what I have taught is largely an echo of what was taught by my grandfathers and other Church leaders many decades ago.

I thought, therefore, that it might be interesting to delve into the teachings of these two Apostles and share some of their words alongside my own as a further witness of the eternal truth of these principles. The quotations from their writings and talks come from family files, Church magazines, general conference reports, and letters written during their numerous missions, some of which were compiled for our family a while ago by Frank Bruno. I have not attempted to include original sources beyond the compilations I have mentioned.

My talks have been edited slightly to make them more readable and to expand my thoughts at specific junctures. The quotes from my grandfathers appear with some minor editing to make them more readable.

In preparing this work, I have seen anew that the course of the Lord truly is "one eternal round" (Alma 37:12) and that the doctrine of the gospel is timely and timeless. It is forever relevant to disciples of the Lord Jesus Christ.

I want to thank Carolyn Hyde, my former secretary; Emily Davis Merrell, my current secretary; and Emily Watts at Deseret Book for their assistance in preparing this book for publication.

I alone am responsible for the content of this book, and I present it with the hope that it may serve the memory of Grandfathers Smith and Ballard well and be a resource for readers that will build and strengthen testimonies that Jesus is the Savior and Redeemer of the world. I am truly happy to share a common witness to the divine truths of the restored gospel of Jesus Christ with my grandfathers.

CHAPTER 1

AN ANCHOR TO THE SOUL

HAVE YOU EVER watched a large ship weigh its anchor? Weighing anchor happens when the ship's anchor rises from the ocean's floor so that the ship can be under way. When the anchor lifts off the ocean floor, it is "aweigh."

My first experience seeing a ship weigh anchor happened during an Atlantic voyage on the *Queen Elizabeth* from the United States to the British Isles when I began my first mission as a young man in 1948. It is fascinating to see and hear the massive links of chain screeching against the metal bow of the ship as the anchor is raised. The metal shanks of the anchor chain are incredibly heavy, but their weight is slight when compared to the total weight of the large ship. Still, if an anchor is placed properly on the sea floor, it can hold a giant ship against ocean currents, heavy winds, and rough seas.

When my wife, Barbara, and I had an opportunity to go on an Alaskan cruise, I was grateful that each time our ship pulled into harbor, we had an anchor to keep the ship close to shore. How awful it would have been to come back from a shore excursion only to discover that our transport home, with all our possessions, was drifting off to open sea away from us. Thankfully, the anchor was secure, and we had peace of mind knowing that whether in a calm harbor or in rough seas, the anchored ship would be safe and secure.

Just as ships need anchors to keep them from drifting away, we need spiritual anchors in our lives if we are not to drift into the sea of temptation and sin.

Faith in the Lord Jesus Christ is the main anchor we must have in our lives to hold us fast during times of challenges, including unexpected health or economic crisis or social and political turbulence. As one of our articles of faith states, "We believe that the first [principle]" of the gospel is: "Faith in the Lord Jesus Christ" (Articles of Faith 1:4). Having faith in our Savior also means having faith in God, His Eternal Father, and in the Holy Ghost (see Articles of Faith 1:1).

This faith must be more than the generic dictionary variety. Our faith, for it to be meaningful and effective and to hold us fast, must be centered in Jesus Christ, His life, and His Atonement, and in the restoration of His gospel to the earth in the last days.

> *I would not belong to a church if I had to confess a Redeemer, a Savior, unless I was convinced beyond a shadow of a doubt that he was, indeed, my Redeemer, and that through him I should, if I kept his commandments, be saved from my sins.*
> —Hyrum Mack Smith

Once I spoke to a group of prospective missionaries. Many of those young men and women had made the decision to serve full-time missions, but others were not certain they should accept a call to serve. I told them that they did not have to decide that night whether to go on a mission. But I said they *did* need to decide whether Joseph Smith knelt in the presence of God, the Father, and His Son, Jesus Christ, "on the morning of a beautiful, clear day, early in the spring of eighteen hundred and twenty."

We read in Joseph's own words:

> After I had retired to the place where I had previously designed to go, having looked around me, and finding myself alone, I kneeled down and began to offer up the desires of

my heart to God. I had scarcely done so, when immediately I was seized upon by some power which entirely overcame me, and had such an astonishing influence over me as to bind my tongue so that I could not speak. Thick darkness gathered around me, and it seemed to me for a time as if I were doomed to sudden destruction.

But, exerting all my powers to call upon God to deliver me out of the power of this enemy which had seized upon me, and at the very moment when I was ready to sink into despair and abandon myself to destruction—not to an imaginary ruin, but to the power of some actual being from the unseen world, who had such marvelous power as I had never before felt in any being—just at this moment of great alarm, I saw a pillar of light exactly over my head, above the brightness of the sun, which descended gradually until it fell upon me.

Excepting only the resurrection of Christ, the vision of 1820 was the most important event in the history of the world. Out of it has come all that we have, because that vision actually occurred.
—MELVIN J. BALLARD

It no sooner appeared than I found myself delivered from the enemy which held me bound. When the light rested upon me I saw two Personages, whose brightness and glory defy all description, standing above me in the air. One of them spake unto me, calling me by name and said, pointing to the other—*This is My Beloved Son. Hear Him!*" (Joseph Smith–History 1:14–17).

If that happened to Joseph, then the question of whether these prospective missionaries should serve a mission or whether they should faithfully keep the Lord's commandments pretty well takes care of itself, doesn't it? If anyone knows, *really knows,* that Heavenly Father and His Beloved Son, Jesus Christ, appeared to and spoke to Joseph Smith as he said They did, the natural outcome of that knowledge should kindle a strong desire to serve God and His Holy Son all the days of the person's life.

When we've done with all arguments—and we have the best in the world—it may and often does fail to convert men. It is only through repentance and individual desire for the truth that the individual testimony can come that Joseph did not lie. That individual testimony alone will withstand all the storms that blow against it.

Go to your Father and ask for that knowledge. You will receive it.

—Melvin J. Ballard

Nothing is more remarkable or important in this life than to know that God our Eternal Father and His Son, Jesus Christ, live and love you.

It follows that it is also important to know They have spoken again from the heavens and have called a modern prophet to teach the fulness of the everlasting gospel once again upon the earth (see Doctrine and Covenants 1:17). That is a glorious thing to know. When you know it, that knowledge affects your life. It influences every major decision you make. It changes the course of your life to a safer one because it provides an anchor that helps hold you fast to the teachings of the gospel despite the evil influences all around you that entice you to drift toward sin and transgression.

I make the same argument for the restoration of the Aaronic Priesthood through John the Baptist and of the Melchizedek Priesthood through Peter, James, and John. Let's be very plain about this. Either the priesthood of God has been restored or it has not. When you know that it has, you have secured your spiritual anchor even more firmly against the turbulence and storms of life.

Similarly, either the Book of Mormon is the word of God and is another testament of Jesus Christ or it is not. Either it is the record of the Lord's dealings with some of the people on the American continent from 600 BC to AD 421 or it is not. Either the Book of Mormon is a translation from gold plates completed by

Joseph Smith under divine guidance or it is not. The issue is that simple and that profound. If the Book of Mormon is, in fact, the word of God, as I testify that it is, then the question of whether we should apply its principles and teachings in our own lives is already decided.

The same simple test applies to our living prophets and Apostles today. Either the current members of the First Presidency and the Quorum of the Twelve Apostles are the legal successors of the Prophet Joseph Smith or they are not. They are either true prophets, seers, and revelators or they are not.

It really is no more complicated than that. If we know these things to be true, we really have no question about how we should live and what we should do with our lives. If we know that we are anchored to "the only true and living church upon the face of the whole earth" (Doctrine and Covenants 1:30), our course is clear. What a marvelous blessing it is to know this!

> *If Joseph Smith was not inspired, if he was not, indeed, a true prophet, how can we account for the fact that he, though an unlearned youth, not educated or graduated from colleges or seminaries, organized a church that is so far superior, in every sense of the term, to any organization yet effected by the learned and the wise?*
>
> —Hyrum Mack Smith

You know how to find out for yourself if these things are true. You understand that you must pray with real intent to receive your personal testimony. You understand that the Holy Ghost "shall teach you all things, and bring all things to your remembrance" (John 14:26). When you know and live these simple truths, they will be a spiritual anchor to help you keep your own life from being "tossed to and fro, and carried about with every wind of doctrine" (Ephesians 4:14).

The author of Hebrews further noted that when we "lay hold

upon the hope set before us," that hope becomes "as an anchor of the soul, both sure and steadfast" (Hebrews 6:18–19).

This reminds me of a scripture found in the Book of Mormon: "Wherefore, whoso believeth in God might with surety hope for a better world, yea, even a place at the right hand of God, which hope cometh of faith, maketh an anchor to the souls of men, which would make them sure and steadfast, always abounding in good works, being led to glorify God" (Ether 12:4).

Let all believers in Christ doubt not, for he delayeth not his coming, neither has he gone afar and forgotten us. Let us all join in continuing the glorious warfare to win this world for Christ, its rightful Ruler.
—Melvin J. Ballard

In another Book of Mormon passage we learn the consequences of not following Christ the shepherd or refusing to be led by the Father: "But now, behold, they are led about by Satan, even as chaff is driven before the wind, or as a vessel is tossed about upon the waves, without sail or anchor, or without anything wherewith to steer her; and even as she is, so are they" (Mormon 5:18).

Becoming anchored to these simple truths and focusing your attention on the lessons of eternity will keep your life at the right place at all times and in all situations, regardless of which way the winds of current worldly trends may be blowing.

Poet Ella Wheeler Wilcox made this observation while she was a passenger on a steamship as she observed that one ship went west and another east in the same wind:

> One ship drives east and another drives west
> With the selfsame winds that blow.
> 'Tis the set of the sails
> And not the gales
> Which tells us the way to go.

Like the winds of the sea are the ways of fate,
As we voyage along through life:
'Tis the set of a soul
That decides its goal,
And not the calm or the strife.

(*Masterpieces of Religious Verse,* n.p.)

Among the most important things you need to know is that you are a true disciple of the Lord Jesus Christ. This assurance will keep everything else in your life in focus and will bring you true happiness and joy; it will become an anchor in your life.

The word *disciple* comes from the Latin word *discipulus*; it means "student" or "learner." Many people think that being a disciple means simply to follow, with an unfortunate connotation of following blindly. Becoming a true disciple of Jesus Christ is nothing of the sort!

Brigham Young observed, "I am more afraid that this people have so much confidence in their leaders that they will not inquire for themselves of God whether they are led by him. I am fearful they settle down in a state of blind self security. Let every man and woman know, by the whispering of the Spirit of God to themselves, whether their leaders are walking in the path the Lord dictates, or not" (*Journal of Discourses,* 9:150).

I bear witness that I know that he lives and that he is the Redeemer of the world. When that day shall come that I may stand in his presence and hear his voice, or like the doubting Thomas, thrust my hand into his wounded side and hands, I shall not know any better then than I do today that he lives and that he has visited the earth in this age in the reintroduction of his glorious Gospel in its fulness and that it shall be triumphant in the earth.
—Melvin J. Ballard

True discipleship requires us to know Jesus Christ, to thoughtfully study the principles of truth, and to find answers to life's questions that can be given only by God. The answers may come through the Holy Ghost directly, or through the inspiration we receive from the scriptures and from our Church leaders.

Please remember that there is a difference between a disciple and a follower. The difference is like the difference between a ship's anchor that is lodged solidly at the bottom of the sea, holding the ship fast, and an anchor that is merely suspended in water because the chain is too short. Such an anchor may appear to be doing its job when the seas are calm, but it serves no purpose during storms or high waves. In fact, a loose anchor can damage a ship in a storm.

Remember these words from the prophet Nephi: "Wherefore, ye must press forward with a steadfastness in Christ, having a perfect brightness of hope, and a love of God and of all men. Wherefore, if ye shall press forward, feasting upon the word of Christ, and endure to the end, behold, thus saith the Father: Ye shall have eternal life" (2 Nephi 31:20).

Every great prophet, including those in the Old Testament, the New Testament, and the Book of Mormon, had to go through the process of becoming a true disciple by coming to an unshakable knowledge of Christ.

Each one had to ask himself just what I am inviting you to ask yourself: "Is Jesus Christ the Son of God, our Eternal Father? Does He live, and does He preside over His Church today?"

The gospel of Christ is the power of God unto salvation unto all those who believe it; but it is not the power of salvation to any man [or woman] who does not believe it. . . . You Latter-day Saints who believe, if you continue in the way of righteousness, shall be redeemed by the blood of Christ and saved and exalted with Him on the right hand of the Father, just as sure as He lives.
—Hyrum Mack Smith

The sure knowledge that Jesus Christ is the Savior and Redeemer of the world provided the courage for Meshach, Shadrach, and Abed-nego to enter a fiery furnace without fear.

Abinadi's knowledge of Christ gave him the power to testify of Christ while being burned to death by the wicked priests of King Noah. The same knowledge that Christ lives gave Nephi the power to endure the incessant insults of his brothers and the strength to suffer until his brothers broke the strong cords that held him bound during a tumultuous storm at sea. Having come to know Christ, Elijah had the power to literally command fire to consume his soggy altar while the priests of Baal watched in awe. An absolute conviction that Jesus Christ is the Messiah gave Samuel the Lamanite the courage to stand on the city wall and bear testimony to the wicked Nephites and to receive protection from their arrows and stones. The brother of Jared was even able to move the mountain Zerin because he knew in his heart of hearts that Jesus Christ is the Son of the living God! (See Daniel 3; Mosiah 13–17; 1 Nephi 18; 1 Kings 18; Helaman 13–16; Ether 12.) The scriptures are filled with righteous acts and testimonies of men and women who came to know for themselves that Jesus is the Christ.

> *I know that Jesus Christ is the Son of the living God, and that he came into the world to offer himself a sacrifice for sin; that he taught the gospel of salvation, and that through the shedding of his blood he became the Redeemer of men. . . . It seems to me that this forms a very substantial foundation upon which to build one's faith in God, and upon which to base one's hope of salvation in the presence of the Father.*
>
> —Hyrum Mack Smith

That same, sure testimony of Jesus can be yours. Testimony and knowledge come as a result of your personal faith and prayers. Ask your Heavenly Father to bless you with faith and courage, and He will help you endure any challenges you may face. He will help you overcome loneliness, feelings of desperation and hopelessness, and setbacks of a personal, emotional, financial, and even spiritual nature. He will strengthen you when you are simply feeling overwhelmed by all of the demands for your time and attention. He will give you the ability to serve faithfully in every assignment you receive from inspired Church leaders.

Your faith and your knowledge of the Restoration of the gospel in these last days will give you the strength to be faithful and true to the covenants you have made with the Lord. That testimony will help you to share your strengths and talents gladly to build up the kingdom of God here on the earth. Your testimony of Jesus Christ is the most important anchor you can have to help hold you, steadfast and immovable, to principles of righteousness, regardless of the challenges and temptations that may come.

[People] must have a true balance or rule that is always dependable, by which they can measure or weigh every particle of information that comes to them. I have discovered that the sure action of my soul is the knowledge I have that God lives; that Jesus is the Christ, and that our Father in Heaven has spoken; that those truths contained in the revelations of God in [the scriptures] are the very eternal truth. I have accepted them as my measuring rod.
—Melvin J. Ballard

The Book of Mormon prophet Ether explained this principle to the people of his day:

> [Ether] could not be restrained because of the Spirit of the Lord which was in him.
>
> For he did cry from the morning, even until the going down of the sun, exhorting the people to believe in God unto repentance lest they should be destroyed, saying unto them that by faith all things are fulfilled—
>
> Wherefore, whoso believeth in God might with surety hope for a better world, yea, even a place at the right hand of God, which hope cometh of faith, maketh an anchor to the souls of men, which would make them sure and steadfast, always abounding in good works, being led to glorify God. (Ether 12:2–4)

The principle is clear. We believe, we hope, we have faith, we act upon that faith by "abounding in good works," and we have an attitude of glorifying God. Then we shall, indeed, have a place at the right hand of God.

A fervent personal testimony of Christ and His Church often comes in simple ways. From my own experiences, I can testify of this. I accepted a call to go to England on a mission when I was nineteen, in 1948. Because of my missionary experience, I became anchored to a testimony of the divine Sonship of Jesus Christ and the reality that He did speak to Joseph Smith, opening the heavens to begin the Restoration of the gospel in these last days. I stood in Hyde Park in London and on many street corners in the British Isles and bore my testimony that God loved the world and sent His Son Jesus Christ (see John 3:16), that Joseph Smith was called of God to be the first modern prophet, that the gospel has been restored in its fulness, and that the priesthood authority to bless mankind is once again upon the earth. The more I bore my testimony, the more it became a part of me.

After I returned home, my testimony gave me the direction and the courage I needed to find the girl of my dreams who would support me in my Church callings and in all my family duties and responsibilities as I would support her in the family duties and callings the Lord would provide her during our lives together. Because of the testimonies we each have, we have been

> *It is worth more to any young man in Israel to have in his very heart and soul a burning conviction, a knowledge that God lives, and that Jesus is the Christ, than to be possessed of much wealth and to be devoid of this blessing. There are few . . . who have gone into the missionary field to discharge this obligation and have done their duty who have not been endowed with an abiding testimony that God does live, and that Jesus Christ is his Son. This in itself is worth everything.*
>
> —Melvin J. Ballard

able to support and encourage each other to live the teachings of the gospel.

My understanding of the gospel has given me guidance on the kind of husband, father, and grandfather I should be. My testimony, gained in my youth, has helped me respond to every call in the Church, from priests quorum adviser, to a young bishop, mission president, and especially the overwhelming call to be a member of the Quorum of the Twelve Apostles. My testimony, obtained a long time ago on the street corners and in the doorways and living rooms of countless modest houses in England, has grown line upon line and precept upon precept until I can stand and testify as a special witness of the Lord Jesus Christ that our Savior lives and that He is the Son of God, our Eternal Father. My life has never been the same since I anchored my soul to Jesus Christ and the truths of His eternal and everlasting gospel.

Now let's return for a moment to the analogy of the ship's anchor, especially the massive chain that holds the anchor secure to the ship. Suppose a beautiful sailing ship had been manufactured from the finest materials and had been reinforced and strengthened for the roughest seas. The mast and sails had been prepared carefully and were sturdy and seaworthy. Suppose the anchor was above standard in size and weight and craftsmanship. But suppose, by some inadvertent error, the chain attached to the anchor was inferior and weak. Visualize what would happen the first time the anchor was lowered or the first time a strong wave tried to push the anchored ship out to sea. If any link of the chain holding the anchor broke, the anchor would be left to rust on the bottom of the ocean floor, and the ship would drift and perhaps be destroyed.

The comparison to our lives is plain. The links in our chain of faith and testimony that enable our personal anchor to keep us safe and secure are the simple doctrine and teachings of the gospel. For example, can you see the value of the gospel link of personal prayer? Thanking your Heavenly Father for your blessings will help you remain secure. Pray for the help you need in your personal life, your family, your education, your career, and your relationships.

Can you see another gospel link in your chain being the Word of Wisdom? By your faithfully living the Lord's law of health, that link in the chain will help you keep your physical body strong. At the same time, you "shall find wisdom and great treasures of knowledge, even hidden treasures," which may be the most important blessing contained in this marvelous revelation (Doctrine and Covenants 89:19).

> *If I keep his commandments and pray in the proper spirit, I shall automatically be brought into perfect accord and tune. My spirit shall hear the message the Father has in answer to my prayer.*
> —Melvin J. Ballard

Good men and women in the world can observe the basic health principles found in the Word of Wisdom and "shall receive health in their navel and marrow to their bones; . . . and shall run and not be weary, and shall walk and not faint" (Doctrine and Covenants 89: 18, 20).

However, as Saints, we have additional promises if we obey the Word of Wisdom, based on our faith in Jesus Christ. We will enjoy the physical blessings found in this revelation and will also enjoy the spiritual blessings associated with observing the Word of Wisdom because we have faith that Jesus Christ is the author of it.

Finding "wisdom and great treasures of knowledge, even hidden treasures" will help you increase your faith in Jesus Christ and faithfulness to His gospel, making you more committed to the Church—anchoring your soul to the restored Church of Jesus Christ.

Another link in the anchor chain is the law of tithing. I believe that paying a full tithe is not a matter of money; rather, it is a matter of faith. You can pay a full tithe regardless of your income if you develop the faith to do so. We must not forget that the Lord's economic plan includes observing the fast and paying an offering. If we pay honest tithes and generous fast offerings the Lord will surely "open . . . the windows of heaven," as He has promised (Malachi 3:10).

How about the links of personal honesty and moral purity in thought and actions? How about the links of Christlike service to others, faithful and consistent weekly worshiping with the Saints at church, and studying the scriptures, to name just a few?

Each link reinforces the other links in the chain, which together help us grow in our discipleship to Jesus Christ. These links of your gospel anchor chain may seem somewhat elementary, but they are as important as the anchor of faith and testimony in Jesus Christ itself.

We must not underestimate the power of simple and fundamental truth. Two Old Testament stories teach this principle. When the children of Israel were plagued with fiery serpents, Moses lifted a serpent of brass to save those who were willing to look upon it (see Numbers 21:6–9). Because looking upon the serpent of brass was so simple, many failed to do so and perished (see 1 Nephi 17:41). At another time, Naaman the Syrian came to Elisha to be healed of leprosy and initially rejected the prophet's instruction to wash himself in the Jordan River because it was not a "great" thing (see 2 Kings 5:8–14).

My experience is that when people become adrift upon the storm-tossed sea, they generally have stopped doing the simple things that would anchor their souls to Christ and His Church.

Years ago one of my missionaries called me seeking an appointment. When he arrived at my office, he told me that he had questions about our Church doctrine and history and was losing his faith in the restored gospel.

I asked him if he had talked to his bishop. He had, but all the

you can in honoring the Lord. Remember that strengthening your testimony is a lifelong process. Look to the Lord for strength to overcome discouragement and hopelessness. Work on one link at a time, and strengthen each until you can feel anchored safely and securely to the gospel of Jesus Christ. I promise you in the name of the Lord that as you honestly deal with yourself by resolving to strengthen any link in your gospel anchor chain that needs strengthening, that through your sincere repentance, you will find spiritual strength and courage to live the gospel as you should.

I testify with all my heart that we cannot fail if we are anchored securely to Jesus Christ and His restored gospel and if we forge strong links in an anchor chain that will hold us fast to the sure and simple principles of the gospel. Commit to serve the Lord and honor Him all the days of your life, and you will be blessed. All of the promises of eternity will be given unto you. This I know!

CHAPTER 2

Be Faithful

The focus of my thoughts in this chapter is on keeping the doctrine and the gospel of Jesus Christ simple. Paul had this concern when he said to the Corinthians: "But I fear, lest by any means . . . [that] your minds should be corrupted from the simplicity that is in Christ" (2 Corinthians 11:3).

In the Book of Mormon, Nephi explained the doctrine and gospel of Christ in simple terms. He said, "For my soul delighteth in plainness" (2 Nephi 31:3). He knew that being clear and concise would be a powerful witness of Jesus Christ and His gospel. Nephi taught:

- "Can we follow Jesus save we shall be willing to keep the commandments of the Father?" (2 Nephi 31:10).
- "And the Father said: Repent ye, repent ye, and be baptized in the name of my Beloved Son" (2 Nephi 31:11).
- "He that is baptized in my name, to him will the Father give the Holy Ghost" (2 Nephi 31:12).
- "And I heard a voice from the Father, saying: Yea, the words of my Beloved are true and faithful. He that endureth to the end, the same shall be saved" (2 Nephi 31:15).
- "For ye have not come thus far save it were by the word of Christ with unshaken faith in him" (2 Nephi 31:19).
- "My beloved brethren, this is the way; and there is none

other way nor name given under heaven whereby man can be saved in the kingdom of God" (2 Nephi 31:21).

- "And now, behold, this is the doctrine of Christ" (2 Nephi 31:21).

Patriarch Hyrum Smith, the older brother of the Prophet Joseph Smith, often taught the need to keep the gospel simple. On one occasion he said:

"The Elders are sent into the world to preach faith, repentance, baptism for the remission of sins, and the laying on of hands for the reception of the Holy Ghost and they should let the mysteries alone . . . and if this generation will not receive the first principles of the gospel and the Book of Mormon, they will receive nothing greater. . . . It is the honest and pure in heart that will harken to the everlasting covenant" (*History of the Church*, 6:320).

The Church of Jesus Christ of Latter-day Saints has a sacred mission to perform in the world. One of the most important features of that mission is to provide new witnesses to this doubting and skeptical generation that Jesus is indeed the Christ, who died for men and is still interested in them and presides under His Father over the destinies of this world.

—Melvin J. Ballard

FAITH IN THE LORD JESUS CHRIST

What is the mission of the Church? It is the mission of our Father in Heaven, defined in this simple statement: "This is my work and my glory—to bring to pass the immortality and eternal life of man" (Moses 1:39). To accomplish His purpose, every soul must be given the opportunity to understand the basic doctrine and gospel of Christ. First, in that doctrine is faith in the Lord Jesus Christ. Our doctrine teaches that we can return to live with our Heavenly Father only by relying on His Son's grace and mercy. When we have faith in Christ, we accept and apply His Atonement and His teachings. We trust Him and what He says. Heavenly Father blesses those who have faith to obey His Son. We believe in Christ, and we follow Him. Remember that He said, "If ye love me, keep my commandments" (John 14:15). That is pretty simple: We show our faith in Him by striving each day to live the gospel. Through our faith in Jesus Christ, He can heal us both physically and spiritually.

Our religion is not a theory; it is a fact. Ours is not a mere confession of faith; it is a great profession with a splendid practice. Ours is not a faith that is dead, being alone; but a live, active faith, closely associated with a conscientious performance of good works.
—Hyrum Mack Smith

I urge you to find some quiet time and ponder the condition of your own faith in the Lord Jesus Christ. Even if it was strong at one time, please consider how strong it is now. In that respect Alma asked the following question: "And now behold, I say unto you, my brethren, if you have experienced a change of heart, and if ye have felt to sing the song of redeeming love, I would ask, can you feel so now?" (Alma 5:26).

Sometimes, our youth, especially our returned missionaries, stop practicing the holy habits they formed at the time of their conversion or in the mission field—behaviors that keep a testimony strong and vibrant. If you know of things you should do to increase your faith, then set a course that will give you the peace and assurance you need to ensure that your faith in Christ will lead you to immortality and eternal life with God.

REPENTANCE

As you have considered your personal faith in God and the Lord Jesus Christ, is there anything that is not what it should be? If there is anything that you know is not consistent with one who has real faith in the Lord Jesus Christ, the next principle to consider is repentance.

We had the opportunity once to go with our adult children and their spouses to the Holy Land. It was a marvelous experience, and I rejoiced at the opportunity to share the sights, sounds, and feelings of the Holy Land with my family. It had a meaningful, positive impact in my own life and in the lives of my family members. But perhaps even more influential was this oft-repeated reminder from my dear wife. "Remember," Barbara would say, "it isn't as important to walk where Jesus walked as it is to walk the way He walked."

All of us, no matter our circumstances, have been invited to walk the way He walked. If we are not doing so, we can choose today to change. That is the essence of repentance.

Our faith and love for the Lord can help us repent or change our thoughts, beliefs, and behaviors that are not in harmony with His commandments and the teachings of His Church. When we repent, we feel godly sorrow; we feel a real desire to stop doing things that are wrong and to increase our efforts to do things that are right. Sincere repentance brings real results in our lives. Most of all, we feel God's forgiveness and His peace in our lives, and our guilt and sorrow are swept away.

> *The purpose of the gospel is to save us from our sins and our weaknesses, through repentance. How often do the Saints pray, "O Father, forgive our sins; overlook our weaknesses, our shortcomings, and our imperfections." The Lord has given the gospel for that very purpose. It is the mission of the gospel to save us from these sins.*
> —Hyrum Mack Smith

If one does not practice and master the principle of repentance, then little habits can become an addiction, and addictions can become so powerful that they destroy us and our family relationships. Make no mistake: all of us are targets of Satan and his minions. He will use every deceitful tactic he has to cause you and me to falter and drift in our commitments and our faithful devotion to the Lord. The prophet Mormon taught that "Satan . . . did blind their eyes and lead them away to believe that the doctrine of Christ was a foolish and a vain thing" (3 Nephi 2:2).

As part of the doctrine of Christ, repentance is necessary to access the cleansing power of Jesus Christ's Atonement, which should be part of our daily lives. Each week we have the blessing of partaking of the sacrament, which helps us to repent and "always remember him and keep his commandments which he has given . . . that [we] may always have his spirit to be with [us]" (Doctrine and Covenants 20:77). We keep our lives clean through sincere repentance and faith in the Lord.

We have seen old men and women who have lived all their lives outside of a knowledge of the truth, being convinced of the error of their way and the necessity of seeking the Lord for a forgiveness of their sins. We have seen them come out of the waters of baptism with their countenances shining, and with a conscience clear before God; and we have known that they had unloaded the weight of their sins, and that God had acknowledged the ordinances we performed in their behalf, that thereby their sins were remitted.
—Melvin J. Ballard

BAPTISM

Baptism by immersion for the remission of sins is the first covenant we make with our Heavenly Father and the Lord Jesus Christ. A covenant is a binding and solemn agreement between God and man. In this ordinance or sacred rite, we show we have willingly entered into a covenant with God, God promises to bless us, and we promise to obey Him.

Remember, Christ set the example for us by being baptized Himself. Like Nicodemus, a ruler of the Jews, we too must understand that "except a man be born again, he cannot see the kingdom of God." Jesus further clarified this doctrine in these words: "Except a man be born of water and of the Spirit, he cannot enter into the kingdom of God" (John 3:3, 5). As we increase our faith in the Lord Jesus Christ, repent of our sins, and honor our baptismal covenant, we are promised the Holy Ghost as a constant companion and trustworthy guide.

THE GIFT OF THE HOLY GHOST

The Holy Ghost is an invaluable gift from a loving Heavenly Father. First, the Holy Ghost testifies of the Father and the Son. Second, the Holy Spirit will "guide you into all truth" (John 16:13). Third, He will "shew you things to come" (John 16:13). Fourth, He will glorify Jesus Christ (see John 16:14). Fifth, He will show the disciples the things of God (see John 16:15).

> *We believe that men [and women] must be baptized by immersion for the remission of their sins, in order that their sins may be washed away and they become clean in the sight of the Lord.*
> —Hyrum Mack Smith

The Holy Ghost helps us recognize the truth, provides spiritual strength, and helps us to do what is right. He also gives us peace and comfort during times of trial or sorrow. The Holy Ghost warns us of spiritual or physical danger. Through the power of the Holy Ghost, we can feel God's love and direction for us. This gift is a foretaste of eternal joy and the promise of eternal life. With the constant companionship of the Holy Ghost, we will know what to do and what *not* to do to remain true to the gospel of Christ.

ENDURE TO THE END

Around the time my wife, Barbara, and I were married, our faithful stake patriarch, who was in his nineties, stood in fast and testimony meeting and said something I have never forgotten. He said, "I pray every night that God will see me safely dead with my testimony burning brightly." After the meeting, I said to him, "Patriarch, of all the people I know, certainly you don't need to worry about that anymore."

He took hold of the lapels of my suit coat, jerked me up so

that our faces were close together, looked me in the eyes, and said these words, "My boy, no one is safe until we have endured faithfully to the very end."

Jesus Christ said it this way: "Now this is the commandment: *Repent,* all ye ends of the earth, and come unto me and be *baptized* in my name, that ye may be sanctified by the reception of the *Holy Ghost,* that ye may stand *spotless* before me at the last day. Verily, verily, I say unto you, this is *my gospel;* and ye know the things that ye must do in my church" (3 Nephi 27:20–21; emphasis added).

We have learned that the greatest gift God has given to us, and, indeed, the greatest gift any of His children ever have or will enjoy, upon this earth, is the companionship of the Holy Ghost. We have learned from contact with Him, from association with Him, that real inspiration and real power are had in the companionship of the Holy Ghost.

—Melvin J. Ballard

THE DOCTRINE OF CHRIST

Nephi summarized the doctrine of Christ, "Wherefore, my beloved brethren, I know that if ye shall follow the Son, with full purpose of heart, acting no hypocrisy and no deception before God, but with real intent, repenting of your sins, witnessing unto the Father that ye are willing to take upon you the name of Christ, by baptism—yea, by following your Lord and your Savior down into the water, according to his word, behold, then shall ye receive the Holy Ghost; yea, then cometh the baptism of fire and of the Holy Ghost; and then can ye speak with the tongue of angels, and shout praises unto the Holy One of Israel. . . . And now, my beloved brethren, I know by this that unless a man shall endure to the end, in following the example of the Son of the living God, he cannot be saved" (2 Nephi 31:13, 16).

How simple the doctrine of Jesus Christ is! How important it is for us to stay on the only pathway defined by God as the way back into His eternal presence. The gospel is the plan of happiness; it is simple and beautiful.

I have reviewed with you the simple yet essential doctrine and gospel of Christ. This is a good time for all of us to pause and be sure we are solidly secure in seeking and living the first principles of the gospel—the doctrine of Christ.

Of course, we should seek learning in every way, for "the glory of God is intelligence" (Doctrine and Covenants 93:36), but we must never, ever cease following the gospel principles that will secure our faith in the Lord Jesus Christ down deep in our hearts and keep it an integral part of us. We always must strive to be better. As we need to repent, let us do so truly and completely. Each Sunday, let us partake of the sacrament with clean hands and pure hearts so we will be worthy of the daily companionship of the Holy Ghost.

I constantly marvel at the reality that our Father in Heaven and His Beloved Son visited Joseph Smith in 1820 and gave him the authority and keys to restore to the earth the fulness of the gospel of Christ. The Book of Mormon and the revelations found in the Doctrine and Covenants repeat over and over again the first principles of the gospel. We have the truth, and we have the holy priesthood to administer the ordinances of eternal salvation for all of God's children. I mention again God's declaration, "This is my work and my glory—to bring to pass the immortality and eternal life of man" (Moses 1:39).

When we consider our individual worth, we might consider a tiny flower seed and all

> *There is no sin, no inherited evil—I care not what it is—that the power of God cannot relieve and eliminate from [our souls]. It can redeem us from the errors and evils of mortality, and raise us without sin unto salvation into the presence of Almighty God. Therefore, no Latter-day Saint is justified in continuing in weaknesses and in imperfections. . . . The gospel was given for the purpose of relieving us of them.*
>
> —Hyrum Mack Smith

of the beauty it brings forth as it grows and blooms. Or, we might consider an apple seed that becomes a tree with hundreds of apples annually. Someone once asked, "How many seeds are in an apple?" And another responded, "No, the question is, how many apples are in a seed?"

Man is a child of God, therefore he partakes of the divine nature of his Father. Within him lie germs of infinite development. Potentially he is a godlike being. Therefore he may rise eternally towards the likeness of his Father in Heaven. Upward, divine, unending is man's destiny.
—MELVIN J. BALLARD

We are the seed or offspring of Almighty God. Just think of your great individual worth as His son or His daughter. The Lord said, "Remember the worth of souls is great in the sight of God" (Doctrine and Covenants 18:10). How often do we stop and think about our infinite and eternal worth as children of God? Such knowledge can give us great comfort and hope in a troubled world where so many of our Father's children are sadly adrift in sin, discouragement, depression, and without understanding of who they really are or the purpose of this mortal life. Many in life feel lost or forgotten. It is our responsibility to find them, love them, and help them come to know they are precious spirit children of God. Just think of the tremendous good that would be accomplished if each of us could help just one lost soul this year to come unto the Lord Jesus Christ.

You are acquainted with the parables of the lost sheep and the lost coin. In each we learn of the "joy . . . in heaven over one sinner that repenteth" (Luke 15:7). Jesus taught these parables to impress upon us the worth of each child of God. The work of saving souls is a labor of love—of finding, caring, befriending, strengthening, teaching, and inviting—one by one! I have experienced that joy. On my mission as a young man in England, I first experienced the joy that comes from sharing my testimony with others. That joy has continued to grow through the years.

Let us make the truth known to others. All that the Lord has given—and He has given freely—let us be willing to give to others. Let us seek for the salvation of the souls of men.

—Hyrum Mack Smith

Each of us needs to be ever watchful so that none of God's children of whom we are aware will ever feel alone, lost, forgotten, unwanted, unneeded, or unaccepted. There are far too many of our members who have lost their way spiritually and need to be rescued by those of us who are anchored to the doctrine of Christ and can save them by sharing with them the divine teachings found in the scriptures and teachings of the modern prophets and apostles.

I believe that when our life is over here and we report to our Father in Heaven, He will be most interested in what we did in bringing the doctrine and gospel to others. I am not sure there is anything more important we can do than teaching our families, and every child of God that we can, the simple truths of the gospel of Christ.

Now, a word of counsel to parents. Remember that the home is the basic unit of the Church and the fundamental classroom for teaching Church doctrine. It is in the home where we must labor to save the souls of our own family members. Parents, please love and nurture your children in righteousness. Teach them the Lord's great plan of happiness both by example and by precept. Praise them often, bless them continually, listen to them when they want to talk to you even if you are busy, encourage them to accomplish good things in their lives, forgive them instantly, and seek their forgiveness when you have done something wrong. No child should ever feel unloved or forgotten by his or her parents and family members. Rather, they should feel love, strength, support, security, guidance, and a refuge from the world when they are in

> *I say to you men of Israel, every man that bears the holy priesthood, every woman that has come to a knowledge of this truth, is one of God's rescue servants, to find and bring into the fold these lost sheep, and preserve not only their bodies, but their spirits from eternal destruction, so that they will not be barred from His presence.*
> —MELVIN J. BALLARD

their homes among members of their family. Home should be a safe place where every child feels valued, appreciated, and loved.

Let us remember that we have been sent here to determine just how committed and dedicated we really are to Heavenly Father's plan. To me, it is exciting to know that we can demonstrate our love by following the commandments and teachings of the Lord Jesus Christ (see John 14:15). Love the gospel of Christ, the simple and basic principles of faith in the Lord Jesus Christ and repentance. Honor the covenants of baptism, live worthy of the Holy Ghost as your companion, and endure to the end. Do this every day, and the Spirit of the Lord will be with you to keep you safely on the pathway that leads to eternal life.

May your family and your personal prayers constantly confirm to you that Father in Heaven loves His children. He wants all to come unto Him through the doctrines of the gospel of His Beloved Son, the Lord Jesus Christ.

CHAPTER 3

"Be Strong in the Lord and in the Power of His Might"

THE SCRIPTURES DESCRIBE OUR DAY as one that will be both "great and dreadful" (Doctrine and Covenants 110:16). The greatness of our day is that we live when the Church of Jesus Christ is restored fully to earth with all of its doctrine, with priesthood authority, and with all of the saving ordinances necessary for any woman or man to receive the full blessings the Lord wants to give His children. We have additional books of scripture that shed further light on the glorious gospel proclaimed in the Old and New Testaments, and we are led by prophets, seers, and revelators. We see the Church fulfilling its divine mission to spread across the world, and we see temples built and operating in many countries.

> *The work of God is going on rapidly in the earth, and we are speeding toward the ultimate consummation of all God's purposes concerning this great work of the latter day. The Saints have every reason to be wonderfully encouraged.*
> —HYRUM MACK SMITH

At the same time, the "dreadfulness" of our day is evident in acts of cruelty in our society, including child, spouse, and elderly abuse, and in the world, where terrorism and barbarity capture the headlines in the news almost every day. All of these point to the painful, dreadful reality that evil is real and rampant in the world. We also live in a day when there are very real and very prevalent spiritual dangers.

President Gordon B. Hinckley had this to say about our day:

> Wonderful as this time is, it is fraught with peril. Evil is all about us. It is attractive and tempting and in so many cases successful. . . . We live in a season when fierce men do terrible and despicable things. We live in a season of war. We live in a season of arrogance. We live in a season of wickedness, pornography, immorality. All of the sins of Sodom and Gomorrah haunt our society. Our young people have never faced a greater challenge. We have never seen more clearly the lecherous face of evil ("Living in the Fulness of Times," 5–6).

The evil one has his recruiting stations open everywhere, enlisting souls in the vain hope that he may yet gain the victory and obtain permanent right of rulership in the earth. . . . These are the forces arrayed against us; but oh, how grateful I am to know that we are not alone in the conflict; we are promised help, aid, and assistance that will make us victorious in the struggle against evil.
—MELVIN J. BALLARD

As the Lord predicted in the preface to the Doctrine and Covenants, we now see the time when "the devil shall have power over his own dominion" (Doctrine and Covenants 1:35). Is it any wonder that some are dismayed and disturbed by what they see? Yet we do not find President Thomas S. Monson or the other apostles and prophets wallowing in despair, nor do we sense even the smallest touch of hopelessness. The opposite is true. As President Hinckley also said: "Now, I do not wish to be an alarmist. I do not wish to be a prophet of doom. I am optimistic. I do not believe the time is here when an all-consuming calamity will overtake us. . . . There is so much of the Lord's work yet to be done. We, and our children after us, must do it" ("The Times in Which We Live," 74).

This hope and optimism come because we know, with absolute certainty, that God is in His heaven and that He is the Lord Omnipotent. God's wisdom and knowledge and power are greater than all the combined forces of evil. He is able to work His will, and His purposes cannot be frustrated (see Doctrine and Covenants 3:1). He has not left you and me to make our way alone in these perilous times. He told His disciples at the Last Supper, "I will not leave you comfortless" (John 14:18). As the footnote in the LDS edition of the Bible states, the word *comfortless* is better translated as "orphans." In other words, Jesus will not leave any of us as orphans. He is watching over His people. Note just a few of the scriptural promises to us:

> *Who can walk safely through the dangers and vicissitudes of life with all these enemies arrayed against us and be successful without the help of the Lord? No wonder He calls upon us to seek Him. He cannot force that spirit upon us nor make us conscious of it, nor give it to us, unless we are willing to seek for it, unless we open our hearts.*
>
> —Melvin J. Ballard

- "He will preserve the righteous by his power" (1 Nephi 22:17).
- "The righteous need not fear; for . . . they shall be saved" (1 Nephi 22:17).
- "The Lord shall have power over his saints, and shall reign in their midst" (Doctrine and Covenants 1:36).
- "[Zion] shall be . . . a land of peace, a city of refuge, a place of safety" (Doctrine and Covenants 45:66).

Those promises are sure. Peace, refuge, safety—that is what our Father wants for His children. But those promises are also conditional. They are extended to those who turn to Him and accept the counsel and guidance He has so freely given us.

Long before the world was formed, Satan and those who followed after him raged against the forces of good and tried to overthrow the work of God. That struggle has not ended, but has merely shifted battlegrounds from there to earth. The war is ruthless and relentless; the objective of the battle is your eternal soul and mine.

The Apostle Paul spoke of how to arm ourselves for this conflict in these very graphic terms: "Be strong in the Lord, and in the power of his might. Put on the whole armour of God, that ye may be able to stand against the wiles of the devil. For we wrestle not against flesh and blood, but against principalities, against powers, against the rulers of the darkness of this world, against spiritual wickedness in high places. Wherefore take unto you the whole armour of God, that ye may be able to withstand in the evil day" (Ephesians 6:10–13).

> *All Latter-day Saints ought to set their faces, as flint, against all manner of evil, and by that example prove to the world that it is possible to live above sin, and not yield.*
> —Hyrum Mack Smith

How do we put on the whole armor of God so that we may, as Paul promises, "be able to withstand in the evil day"?

For my purposes, I like to think of this spiritual armor not as a solid piece of metal molded to fit the body, but more like chain mail—apparently invented by the Celts in Europe and then eventually spread to other parts of the world. Chain mail, or *maille*, consists of dozens of tiny pieces of steel fastened together to allow the user greater flexibility without losing protection. I like it as a metaphor for our spiritual armor because it has been my experience that there is not *one* great and grand thing we can do to arm ourselves spiritually. True spiritual power lies in numerous smaller acts woven together in a fabric of spiritual fortification that protects and shields from all evil.

It is a common expression to talk about the "chinks" in a person's armor. The definition of the word *chink* is "a crack, a cleft . . .

a narrow opening" (*Random House Dictionary*, 360). Should an arrow strike exactly one of the chinks in one's armor, a fatal wound could result. I suggest six ways we can protect ourselves by eliminating any chinks or gaps in our personal spiritual armor:

1. RELY ON THE PROTECTIVE POWER OF PRAYER

Numerous teachings about the importance of prayer are found throughout the scriptures, but one specifically ties prayer to power, especially the power to resist temptation. Modern revelation teaches, "Pray always, that you may come off conqueror; yea, that you may conquer Satan, and that you may escape the hands of the servants of Satan that do uphold his work" (Doctrine and Covenants 10:5).

> *Prayer has unlocked the door that has brought us all our blessings.*
> —Melvin J. Ballard

What a wonderful promise! In this spiritual warfare that rages over individual souls, that is what we want more than anything else—to conquer Satan and to escape the hands of evil men and women who carry out his work. I cannot stress too highly the protective power that comes into our lives through earnest, humble, consistent, yearning prayer.

I know you believe that, but in the hectic, pressure-filled schedule you face, I also know how easy it is to let prayer slip. Chances are you sometimes hit the snooze button on your alarm clock, thinking you can eke out another minute or two of sleep, then jerk awake realizing that you are going to be late for school or work. On such mornings, prayer gets pushed aside, perhaps with a feeble promise to yourself that you will do better tomorrow. Put the alarm clock where you can't reach it from the bed; that will solve this problem. Sometimes you return home late at night, exhausted and eager to collapse into bed. You may go through the motions of prayer in a perfunctory and superficial manner, but that is not the kind of prayer that helps us conquer Satan.

Perhaps you live in an apartment with roommates, and the television or the music may be on day and night. Maybe you have little children in your home, or teenagers, and people talk loudly enough that even in your bedroom you can hear them clearly. There is laughter, there is noise, and there are interruptions. In such circumstances, it is a challenge to find a time and a place where you can be alone with your Heavenly Father. The Savior spoke of entering into our closets to pray (see Matthew 6:6), suggesting the importance of privacy and quiet when we talk with God. For most people, their closets will not allow this to happen, so you need to find a time and place where you can be alone with the Lord and pour out your heart to Him, that you might add strength and power to your spiritual life. Every honest and sincere prayer adds another piece to chain-mail armor.

I would rather go blind all the rest of my days, than to be spiritually blind, and to be denied the glorious privilege that comes from the light that descends upon my soul as I seek my Father in prayer.
—Melvin J. Ballard

Perhaps some of you have slipped into patterns of behavior that you know in your heart are displeasing to the Lord. You feel unworthy and ashamed to approach your Father in Heaven. "I'll repent first," you say to yourselves, "and then I'll begin saying my prayers again." I tell you with all soberness that those thoughts are not from the Lord; rather, they come from the evil one. Nephi said it very clearly: "The evil spirit teacheth not a man to pray, but teacheth him that he must not pray" (2 Nephi 32:8). It is when we are lost in the mists of darkness and cannot find our way that we most desperately need the influence of the Lord. Nowhere in all of the scriptural injunctions on prayer do we find the suggestion that we must first be perfect to communicate with God.

Seek for more truth; put yourselves in a position to receive more truth; and God stands willing and anxious to still pour out upon us a knowledge of greater truths than we at present can conceive of.
—Hyrum Mack Smith

Let me offer a further word of caution. I often hear people say, "I told the Lord this" or "I told the Lord that." Be careful not to "tell" Him; rather, humbly seek and ask your Heavenly Father for guidance and direction. The Lord said, "Be still, and know that I am God" (Psalm 46:10). After pouring out our hearts in sincere prayer, we may need to listen for His response more often than we do. Prayer should express yearning and should be filled with gratitude.

One of the most important ways to clothe yourself in the armor of God is to make sure that prayer—earnest, sincere, consistent prayer—is part of your daily life.

2. RELY ON THE PROTECTIVE POWER OF THE SCRIPTURES

There is another very direct and specific promise about how to gain spiritual power and protection. When Nephi's brothers asked him what the meaning of the rod of iron was, Nephi explained: "I said unto them that it was the word of God; and whoso would hearken unto the word of God, and would hold fast unto it, they would never perish; neither could the temptations and the fiery darts of the adversary overpower them unto blindness, to lead them away to destruction" (1 Nephi 15:24).

Isn't that the protective power we all seek? We want to resist the temptations of Satan and not be blinded by his cunning ways. Knowledge gained through our study of the scriptures teaches us how to get protection from the devil for ourselves.

Note the choice of verbs Nephi used. He did not talk about merely reading the scriptures. He did not suggest that we study only the word of God. He said that we must "hearken" to the word of God and "hold fast" to it. How do we "hearken" and "hold fast" to the word?

When [we have] received . . . the Holy Ghost as a gift from God, [we have] received a comforter to [our] soul, a light to [our] path, a spirit that giveth understanding and knowledge, that brightens the mind, quickens the intellect, and gives a proper comprehension of the things of God that have been revealed through the prophets, and are written in the holy scriptures. [Men and women] with this spirit, reading the scriptures, will understand them.
—Hyrum Mack Smith

Nephi implies that we need to do much more than cursory, occasional reading of the scriptures. We not only need to read and study and learn the scriptural content but also must hearken to it, follow the principles taught therein, and cling to those principles as though our very lives depended on it—which, if we are speaking of spiritual life, is literally true.

To read, understand, live, and love the scriptures is one of the most important things we can do to protect ourselves from the "fiery darts of the wicked" (Ephesians 6:16).

Alma taught that there is great power in the word (see Alma 31:5), but this power won't come by simply having the Book of Mormon on your nightstand. It won't come by having others bear testimony of the truthfulness of the scriptures. They cannot hold fast to the iron rod for you; only you can do that.

I can understand why scripture study can so easily be neglected. You have many demands pulling at you. But I plead with you to make time for immersing yourself in the scriptures. Couple scripture study with your prayers. Half an hour each morning privately studying, pondering, and communicating with your Heavenly Father can make an amazing difference in your life. It will give you increased success in your daily activities. It will bring increased alertness to your mind. It will give you comfort and rock-steady assurance when the storms of life descend upon you.

Here are some practical suggestions that I hope will help you derive greater power from your study of the scriptures:

- If possible, set a consistent time and place to study when you can be alone and undisturbed.
- Always have a marking pencil ready as you study. Make notations in the margins. Write cross references. This can also be done with scripture applications for your smart phones and tablets if you choose to study the scriptures in an electronic format. Make the scriptures yours by marking them.
- Commit yourself to study for a set amount of time rather than to just read a chapter or a certain number of pages. Sometimes a single verse or short passage will take the entire time as you think about it and consider what it means for you.
- Study topically as well as chronologically. Both approaches have merit, but we need to go the Topical Guide or the Index from time to time and read all the Lord has said on repentance or faith or some other principle.
- Take time to ponder, reflect, meditate, and pray about what you read. Ask yourself questions such as "What can I learn from this passage that will help me come unto Christ and be more like Him?"

> *Read the scriptures often and pray for wisdom. Read a whole book through, whenever possible, so as to get a general view of the plan and contents. Read it again and again. He who shall do this will gradually obtain the sense in which the particular author uses the words and phrases that [are employed].*
> —Hyrum Mack Smith

One thing I have learned in life is how frequently the Lord answers our questions and gives us counsel through the scriptures.

It is not unusual for one of us in the Quorum of the Twelve to say, "I saw this teaching more clearly than ever before in this verse of scripture." Let us then go to the Lord in prayer, pleading for help or answers, and those answers will come as we open the scriptures and begin to study them. Sometimes it is as though a passage hundreds or thousands of years old was dictated specifically to answer our question.

Remember the promise of the Lord: If you "hold fast" to the word of God, the fiery darts of the adversary will not penetrate your chain mail. Your spiritual armor will be strong.

3. DRAW ON THE PROTECTION OF THE MERCIFUL GRACE OF GOD

The grace of God is one of the most important tools we are given to fortify ourselves in time of peril. As the Lord promised us through the prophet Moroni, "If men come unto me I will show unto them their weakness. I give unto men weakness that they may be humble; and my grace is sufficient for all men that humble themselves before me; for if they humble themselves before me, and have faith in me, then will I make weak things become strong unto them" (Ether 12:27).

There are several interesting things about that scripture. First is the fact that the Lord gives us weaknesses—not sins, but weaknesses—so that we may be humble. Think about that for a moment. If we were perfect in every respect, it would be hard to be humble. Even in specific things, humility comes harder to those who are very strong in one area or another. The woman or man who is remarkably beautiful or handsome can easily become proud of her or his appearance. An accomplished musician or athlete may not show any interest in someone much less gifted. A brilliant scholar may look down in condescension on those less intellectually blessed. Conversely, our weaknesses help us to be humble.

Then comes the promise. If we are willing to humble ourselves, then, as it says, "my grace is sufficient." In the Bible Dictionary, *grace* is defined as "an enabling power." Can you see the significance of that promise?

One of the signs of our day is how frequently we use the word *addiction* to describe destructive behavior. We talk about being addicted to alcohol, about drug addiction, and of addiction to pornography. These are all insidious and powerful evils. Jesus warned His disciples that "whosoever committeth sin is the servant of sin" (John 8:34). Alma used a similar metaphor when he warned us about "the chains of hell" (Alma 12:11).

> *I believe we are willing to receive the word of the Lord and that we will repent of our sins and overcome these evils that we have allowed ourselves to become addicted to and which were prompted by the false spirits that have gone abroad in the world to deceive men.*
>
> —Hyrum Mack Smith

One of the most devastating effects of sin is that it weakens you, binds you, and brings you down to slavery. The grace of God and of His Son, the Lord Jesus Christ, is the answer to that predicament. If you will but humble yourself and turn to Them, Their grace, Their enabling power, can not only help you throw off the chains of sin but actually turn your weaknesses into strengths.

How I long to have the reality of that promise sink into your heart! Are you struggling with some sin or weakness? It can be something as simple as not having the willpower to rise in the morning early enough to have time for scripture study and prayer. It can be something so powerful, such as Internet pornography or lack of self-control, that you feel like you have been pulled down into an abyss and there is no hope for you. Do you find yourself hating what you are doing but not able to find the willpower to turn away from it? Then reach out and humble yourself. The Lord's enabling power is sufficient to change your heart, to turn your life, to purge your soul. But you must make the first move, which is to humble yourself and realize that only in God can you find deliverance.

4. WATCH YOURSELVES

King Benjamin, in his last great address to his people, counseled and warned them: "But this much I can tell you, that if ye do not watch yourselves, and your thoughts, and your words, and your deeds, and observe the commandments of God, . . . ye must perish. And now, O man, remember, and perish not" (Mosiah 4:30).

I have thought much about what King Benjamin meant by that phrase and about its implications for each of us. Here are some of the things I have concluded:

> *If our eyes were only opened to see the powers that are about us, that seek to influence us, we could not have the courage to walk alone and unassisted.*
> —Melvin J. Ballard

Often in the scriptures the Lord speaks of watchmen on the towers and of watchtowers (see, for example, Doctrine and Covenants 101:12, 43–60). A watchtower is generally raised so that someone can climb to the top and see a great distance. In this way, people working outside of the city walls in the fields and vineyards are alerted to danger or threat much sooner than they would otherwise be, and are provided the time to make their way back into the safety of the city before the enemy descends upon them (see Ezekiel 33:1–6).

The same principle holds true in our lives. We can raise watchtowers that help us deal with threats before they actually descend upon us. Let me give some examples. Bishops often hear in confessions of moral transgression a statement something like this: "I was so sure that I would never be caught in this problem. Somehow we got carried away, and then it was too late." The physical and emotional drives associated with physical affection are powerful, lowering the will to resist and often sweeping people on to things they will later deeply regret.

It is not enough to simply say, "I will never do that." This is an excellent example of where we need to watch ourselves. The wise couple will build watchtowers to protect themselves from being swept away during their courtship. These are simple things, such as limiting the time they are alone together; strictly avoiding dark, isolated places; and setting strict limits on the bounds of their physical affection. To wait until you are caught up in the passion of the moment to start building watchtowers is to wait until the enemy is upon you, and often it is too late.

> *The enemy of our souls is alert and awake. He is trying by new methods to corrupt men and women. There is not a man or a woman that lives that shall not be tried, whose position shall not be assailed, and if Satan can make an entrance he will endeavor to capture that soul.*
>
> —Melvin J. Ballard

I know that some are struggling with the tenacious power of pornography, including the easily obtained pornography found on the Internet. You hide your use from family members because you know it is wrong. You would be embarrassed if detected.

Scientific studies have revealed the addictive nature of pornography and the damage it causes in our relationships with real people, including spouses, parents, and children. Those addicted to pornography don't need to read the scientific reports; they know they are addicted because they cannot stop consuming it, no matter how often they say they will stop.

Some of you come away from such encounters ashamed and sickened, vowing that you will never again allow yourself to give in to that temptation. Such determination is good, but you need to take intervening action when you are calm and away from the influence of those images.

Let me give you some suggestions how to set boundaries.

1. Move your desktop computer into a room where there is always the possibility of someone walking in on you.
2. Make sure the monitor faces the room so that others can see what it is you are doing on the screen at any time.
3. Do not surf the Internet late at night or when you are alone, especially when using portable devices such as a laptop, tablet, or smart phone.
4. Ask someone you trust to regularly check your history on the device you commonly use to access the Internet. Promise not to clear the history of the websites you have examined.
5. Purchase and use inexpensive software programs that screen out most pornographic sites and eliminate most unsolicited, provocative emails.

Take action when you are strong so that if you are tempted, you will have armed yourself. Such precautions will make it much more difficult to fall. This kind of help may be the extra help and support you need to avoid looking at web pages that are inappropriate.

If you have found yourself already addicted to this spiritually and emotionally deadly plague, a friend, family member, or Church leader may help and support you in overcoming your addiction. However, as with alcoholism, their assistance may not be enough—you may need professional help and counseling. Don't be afraid to seek help now before you destroy those relationships that are most important to you.

It is such a logical decision to prepare for danger or discomfort in the natural world. Mountain climbers are very careful to pack the proper gear. Arctic explorers do not wait until the blasts of subzero winds strike them to decide what clothing they need. So why don't we do the same in our spiritual lives?

These are but a few examples of how you can take preventive and protective action in advance so you are covered with the full armor of God. Remember the old saying, "It is far better to prepare and prevent than it is to repair and repent."

5. DON'T WASTE THE DAYS OF YOUR PROBATION

As my father lay on his deathbed, he expressed great apprehension about dying and manifested some despondency. This was very unlike him. After a while, I took his hand and looked him in the eye and said, "Father, do you really believe what you have been teaching all of your life?" When he responded, "You know I do," I then asked him what it would be like on the other side. We discussed who would greet him first. We talked about his father, Elder Melvin J. Ballard, and his mother, Martha A. Jones Ballard. We discussed his siblings who had preceded him in death. As we talked, a transformation came over my father. He began to bask in the reality of the light of Jesus Christ and the mission of the Son of God. He became excited, almost eager to get there to become busy in the work of the Lord on the other side.

If you would have a strong spirit which has dominion over the body, you must see to it that your spirit receives spiritual food and spiritual exercise.

—MELVIN J. BALLARD

It was a tremendous blessing for me to hold the hand of that dear man, my beloved father, and counsel with him and bask in the light of Christ.

One day, each of us will be in this position, thinking back on our lives and ahead to the transition to the other side. Hopefully, we can face this moment like my father ultimately did, looking forward to the future. However, some might not be as peaceful in this moment of reflection. The scriptures say, "Wo unto him that has the law given, . . . that wasteth the days of his probation" (2 Nephi 9:27).

How do we "waste" the days of our probation? Turning to sin is surely part of it, but there is another, more subtle way, a way that may not seem evil at all. The Lord gives a similar warning in these words: "Thou shalt not idle away thy time, neither shalt thou bury thy talent that it may not be known" (Doctrine and Covenants 60:13).

Why would I speak of that with you? Because one of the ways Satan lessens your effectiveness and weakens your spiritual strength is by encouraging you to spend large blocks of your time doing things that matter very little. I speak of such things as sitting for hours on end watching television, videos, YouTube, and Netflix; playing computer games; endlessly surfing the Internet; spending more time with your Facebook friends than with family and friends who live with you, or devoting huge blocks of time to sports, games, or other recreational activities.

> *Let us see to it that we do not lose the Spirit of God by lapsing into indifference, into neglect of duty, into failure to pray. . . . One step leads to another, until by and by the Spirit is grieved and will no longer strive with us.*
>
> —Hyrum Mack Smith

Now, don't misunderstand me. These activities are not wrong in and of themselves (unless, of course, you are watching salacious programs or seeking out pornographic images on the Internet). Games, sports, recreational activities, and even television can be relaxing and rejuvenating, especially in times when you are under stress or heavily scheduled. You need activities that help you to unwind and rest your mind. It is healthy to go onto the soccer field or the basketball or volleyball court and participate in vigorous physical activity. Again I say, these things are not wrong in and of themselves.

No, I speak of letting things get out of balance. It is not watching television but watching television hour after hour, day and night, that becomes a problem. Does not that qualify as idling away your time? What will you say to the Lord when He asks what you have done with the precious gift of life and time? Surely you will not feel comfortable telling Him that you were able to pass the 100,000-point level in a challenging video game.

> *The Prophet Joseph Smith thought it not a dishonorable thing to engage in play. It is reported that many times when he defeated an antagonist in a religious discussion he gave his opponent another chance to win by offering to wrestle, pull stakes, or engage in some other play activity.*
>
> —MELVIN J. BALLARD

This idea of not wasting the days of our probation has deeper significance. One of the greatest challenges of this life is the ordering of priorities. If we do not do this wisely, then things that matter most in life are at the mercy of things that matter least. Too many people are willing to sit back and let life just happen to them. It takes time to develop the attributes that will help you to be a well-balanced person.

Remember, you *can* be exalted without a college degree. You *can* be exalted without conforming to current cultural ideas about appropriate body image. You *can* be exalted without having a successful and financially rewarding career. You *can* be exalted if you are not famous. So focus the best that you can on those things in life that will lead you back to the presence of God—keeping all things in their proper balance.

These are the days of your probation. This time is a precious window of opportunity to prepare for your future. Do not waste this time away. Record the things that matter most to you; make a list of the goals that you hope to accomplish in life and the things that are required if they are to become a reality for you. Plan and prepare and then do.

6. REMEMBER THAT REVERENCE INVITES REVELATION

Being reverent invites the spirit of revelation and is of great importance in spiritually fortifying ourselves. A lack of reverence opens up not just chinks in our chain-mail armor but great gaps of vulnerability.

We should receive reproof with the same spirit that we receive commendation. We are sorry, to be sure, that we have to be reproved because of neglect of duty, but if neglect does prevail among us, then we need to be reproved, and it is my belief that this people will be more faithful . . . than they perchance have been before.
—Hyrum Mack Smith

In a modern revelation, the Lord declared that "your minds in times past have been darkened because . . . you have treated lightly the things you have received" (Doctrine and Covenants 84:54). That is a recurring theme in the revelations. "Trifle not with sacred things," the Lord warned Oliver Cowdery (Doctrine and Covenants 6:12).

In a time of peril and danger, the last thing we need is to have our minds darkened. And yet we have seen a great increase in how the world treats lightly and often offensively things of deep value. Media figures joke and poke fun at even the most sacred things. Television sitcoms, as they are called, show people constantly engaging in crude, rude, immoral, and cruel banter.

When we speak of reverence, we are talking about much more than mere quietness at our meetings. Reverence is an attitude of mind and heart. It involves a keen sense of God's majesty and infinite goodness and of our unworthiness and need for Him and His redeeming grace. It includes a profound sense of the sacred and a desire to honor and protect it.

President Boyd K. Packer said: "Reverence invites revelation. . . . No one of us can survive in the world of today, much less in what it soon will become, without personal inspiration. The spirit of reverence can and should be evident in every organization in the Church and in the lives of every member" ("Reverence Invites Revelation," 21–23).

Without belaboring that point, may I say just a few things to consider? As leaders, we see some patterns relating to reverence that, if not corrected, may open up chinks in your spiritual armor. For example, we have noticed a growing trend in the Church to arrive late at sacrament, Relief Society, and priesthood meetings. Bishops and stake presidents report some members coming in as late as half an hour after the meeting has started. Occasionally, there may be a legitimate excuse for not arriving on time (such as an emergency appendectomy), but in most cases, it is because people simply plan poorly or may not understand how important it is to arrive on time. The ideal would be to arrive five or ten minutes early so you can sit in the chapel quietly listening to the prelude music and preparing yourself to worship. Our sacrament meetings belong to the Savior. When we arrive late, it not only interrupts the reverence of others but is a sign that we do not understand how important it is for us to prepare to worship Him.

Far too often we see people who persist in whispering during the administration of the sacrament. Their minds and hearts are obviously not focused on the emblems of which we partake. It is difficult for me to comprehend how anyone who has an understanding of and an appreciation for the Atonement of the Lord Jesus Christ could allow this to happen.

Another distraction during the administration of the sacrament is modern devices such as cell phones and tablets. I encourage you to put those devices completely away during that most sacred ordinance. Surely, during those few minutes, you can focus on the

Atonement of the Savior as you seek the Spirit of the Lord to bless you for the coming week. Consider putting your smart phone or your tablet in airplane mode for the entire Sunday block. You will still have your scriptures, general conference talks, hymnbook, and manuals, but you will not be distracted by incoming text messages or push notifications.

Here are a few other concerns:

- Each human soul is precious in the sight of God (see Doctrine and Covenants 18:10). To belittle or ridicule someone who has traits that you view as peculiar or to speak in a demeaning manner of members of the opposite sex is offensive to God. We must ask ourselves if we say or do anything that demeans any child of God. An additional step may include asking someone we trust entirely, someone we know loves us, if any of our words or actions could hurt another precious soul.
- Gossip and the passing on of half-truths or untruths about others will likewise cause you to lose power.
- Joking about sacred things or speaking of them in inappropriate places or in inappropriate ways is a sign of irreverence. Off-color language or swearing is offensive and wrong.
- The intimate relationship between a man and woman is one of the most sacred aspects of the Lord's plan. Vulgar jokes and coarse comments about this relationship deeply offend the Spirit.

It is at the sacrament meeting, when you see the emblems of the broken body and the spilt blood being prepared, that is the time for every man and woman to go into secret conference with himself or herself and discover whether or not they are in sin and transgression, whether they have yielded to the tempter, whether there are things that they need to repent of, and if so, to cleanse themselves and purify their souls.
—Melvin J. Ballard

By carefully cultivating an attitude of reverence in these matters, you will strengthen the power and the influence the Spirit has in your life. Remember, "reverence invites revelation."

> *We will continue to believe and to practice the gospel; we will continue to be obedient and to serve God; we will continue to love our neighbor as ourselves, to return good for evil, to give a blessing for a cursing; we will continue in the straight and narrow path which leadeth unto eternal life, in spite of all that the adversary of the souls of men can do.*
> —Hyrum Mack Smith

The Lord has given us specific doctrines and principles that show us how to clothe ourselves in the armor of God so that we can stand against the powers of evil. I have tried to suggest a few ways to incorporate gospel principles into your life. In most cases, we are not talking about massive changes of behavior. As with chain mail, you need simply to add small, individual pieces of armor each day through praying, studying the scriptures, focusing on things that really matter, and acting in a reverent manner.

We should all be seeking to live eternally with our Heavenly Father and our Savior, the Lord Jesus Christ. All they have can be ours. What they offer far excels any earthly accomplishment. So go forward, keeping the commandments of God and following the admonition of the Apostle Paul: "Be strong in the Lord, and in the power of his might. Put on the whole armour of God, that ye may be able to stand against the wiles of the devil" (Ephesians 6:10–11).

CHAPTER 4

The Importance of Each Soul

When I was first called, at the age of twenty-seven, to be a bishop's counselor, I was placed over the Scouting program. We were in need of a Scoutmaster, and unfortunately there were not many active, qualified people available. I almost wore out the ward roster going over it again and again looking for someone I could call. Finally, after I had fasted and prayed mightily, a name came to mind, and I presented it at our next meeting. The bishop informed me he could not call the man of my choice because he was inactive and had a Word of Wisdom problem. I explained he was the only man who had enough knowledge of Scouting to make this work. Someone suggested that the bishop should call on him and get him active.

I had great faith in the bishop. We went one evening, and the bishop knocked on the door. This good man came to the door. The bishop said to him, "We are the bishopric. We have come to visit with you, and Brother Ballard has something he would like to ask you." With that, the bishop stepped back and pushed me forward.

I looked this good brother in the eye and hesitated but a moment before saying, "We need you to be the Scoutmaster. Will you come to church? Will you be active? We need you in this calling."

He was quite surprised, as he had not been active for some

time, and he asked for time to think it over. I returned a few days later, and he asked me if I really thought he could do it. I assured him that I did, and he accepted the call.

Things did not go perfectly at first, and he had a moment where he slipped back into his past behavior. However, through encouragement and love from those around him, he fulfilled his calling and returned to full activity in the Church. He started paying a full tithe and ultimately took his family to the temple to be sealed.

If I live to be a thousand years old, I'll never lose the vision of that good man and his wife kneeling at the altar. This man's father was a very active member of the Church. He had six sons, but none of them were active, except this one. When the family entered the sealing room, and we watched as the children lined up according to age, took each other's hands, and placed their hands on top of their parents' hands, everyone in the room was in tears.

Afterward, the man's father came to me, put his arms around my neck, and wept as he told me, "Bishop, there isn't any way to tell you and your ward members how much it means to me and my wife to have one of our boys safely in the temple of the Lord."

We have a great need to move the work of the Lord forward faster. Thousands of people live in every region of the world who will join the Church if all of you members and missionaries increase your faith and share what you know to be true. And additional thousands within the Church membership need to be fellowshipped back into full activity and participation. These are beloved sons and daughters of our Heavenly Father, who, like the father of this faithful Scoutmaster, wants His children safely in the temple of the Lord.

Remember these declarations of the Lord: "Behold, I sent you out to testify and warn the people, and it becometh every man who hath been warned to warn his neighbor" (Doctrine and Covenants

88:81). "For there are many yet on the earth among all sects, parties, and denominations, who are blinded by the subtle craftiness of men, whereby they lie in wait to deceive, and who are only kept from the truth because they know not where to find it" (Doctrine and Covenants 123:12).

> *No generation of men and women have ever had a more serious obligation upon them than the members of this Church—to let the whole world know that God has spoken in this hour of warning, and has offered the means of escape for all His children. It is an obligation that rests upon, not only the man who has a son or daughter whom he sends into the mission field, but upon every man and woman.*
> —Melvin J. Ballard

The Book of Mormon teaches that, following their conversion, the sons of King Mosiah—Ammon, Aaron, Omner, and Himni—desired of their father "that they might . . . go up to the land of Nephi that they might . . . impart the word of God to their brethren, the Lamanites—that perhaps they might bring them to the knowledge of the Lord their God, and convince them of the iniquity of their fathers . . . that they might also be brought to rejoice in the Lord their God. . . . Now they were desirous that salvation should be declared to every creature, for they could not bear that any human soul should perish" (Mosiah 28:1–3). Many of you dear Saints must have the same feelings when you consider how precious is one soul.

As you know, Mosiah, their father, prophet, and king, granted them this wish. They spent the next fourteen years on a mission declaring the word of God among the Lamanites. Through their loving and devoted service of sharing the gospel, they were successful in bringing thousands unto a true knowledge of God and eventual salvation to their souls. Their peace and joy were the great reward for their faithful service.

I have experienced that same joy when someone joins the

Church through some small effort on my part. Hopefully, you too have experienced this. If not, ask yourself, What is the worth of one human soul, and what more can I do to reach more of them?

From the *Guide to the Scriptures* we read: "All persons are spirit children of God. He cares about each of His children and considers each one important. Because they are His children, they have the potential to become like Him. Therefore, they are of great worth" (s.v. "soul").

One of the significant truths restored to the earth through the Prophet Joseph Smith is that every person who has ever lived or will yet live upon the earth is a child of God. Each will have the opportunity to know and then to accept or reject Heavenly Father's eternal plan of salvation. The work of this latter-day dispensation is that of saving souls of both the living and the dead.

President Wilford Woodruff told of visitations with the Prophet Joseph Smith after the Prophet's death. He said the following:

> *All of us may have a knowledge that this is the one and only religion in all the wide world of which it can be said, "all they have is true." Yet how gladly we would extend it to everyone else! How gladly we would give to others that which we have received, and how assiduously are we working for the salvation of men, as is evidenced by the hundreds upon hundreds of [missionaries] sent forth to proclaim repentance and salvation to the world!*
>
> —Hyrum Mack Smith

> Joseph Smith continued visiting myself and others up to a certain time, and then it stopped. The last time I saw him was in heaven. In the night vision I saw him at the door of the temple in heaven. He came to me and spoke to me. He said that he could not stop to talk with me because he was in a hurry. The next man I met was Father Smith; he could not talk with me because he was in a hurry. I met half a dozen brethren who had held high positions on earth, and none of

them could stop to talk with me because they were in a hurry. I was much astonished. By and by, I saw the Prophet again and I got the privilege of asking him a question.

"Now," said I, "I want to know why you are in a hurry. I have been in a hurry all my life; but I expected my hurry would be over when I got into the Kingdom of Heaven, if I ever did."

Joseph said, "I will tell you, Brother Woodruff. Every dispensation that has had the priesthood on the earth and has gone into the celestial kingdom has had a certain amount of work to do to prepare to go to the earth with the Savior when He goes to reign on earth. Each dispensation has had ample time to do this work. We have not. We are the last dispensation, and so much work has to be done, and we need to be in a hurry in order to accomplish it."

There is something else to learn after we leave this earth, and I rejoice in the anticipation of further and greater knowledge concerning the things I do not now understand. The Lord touched Joseph's understanding when He likened His kingdom to a man having a field, who sent a group of workers to his part of the field and gave them instructions what to do and told them He would visit them in their hour and in their time.
—Melvin J. Ballard

And then Wilford Woodruff concluded, "Of course, that was satisfactory with me, but it was new doctrine to me" ("Discourse Delivered at the Weber Stake Conference," 642–43).

From this urgent call to action of the Prophet Joseph, it seems to me that today all of us should be in a greater hurry to share the gospel with the precious children of our Heavenly Father. Here are four things that will help each one of us do our part:

First, we need to strengthen homes and families—first our own and then the families of other Church members. Remember that the home is the fundamental classroom for teaching the doctrine of Christ. It is in the home where we must labor to save the souls of our own family members.

Second, we need to strive to perfect and save our own souls and the souls of other Church members. We help each other to receive all of the ordinances of the gospel and to make and keep the associated covenants. We help, as leaders and teachers in the priesthood and auxiliary organizations of the Church, to strengthen members and families. We provide loving and supportive watch care as home and visiting teachers. We help those in need—especially the widows, orphans, lonely, disabled, sick, poor, and otherwise disadvantaged. We care for and encourage our children and youth. And we strive to live exemplary lives of obedience and service so that those around us might draw strength from us. That sounds like a lot, but when you think about it really carefully, it is following the Savior's simple but profound statement, "If ye love me, keep my commandments" (John 14:15).

Third, we should strive to save the souls of those not yet members of the Church. We do this by creating gospel-sharing homes wherein we can teach our friends and neighbors the truths of the restored gospel of Jesus Christ and the great plan of redemption. We watch for opportunities to serve one another. Remember to invite those who are not members of the Church to join you and other Church members in Church and community service projects. They will often agree to come. And as you work side by side, you can fellowship and encourage so they will feel your love for them.

For missionaries to become powerful teachers, they need many opportunities to teach. The ward council should see that they teach every single day. If they have no appointment to do so, then have them teach the less-active members or other families in the ward because the missionaries thereby improve their teaching skills by teaching every day. Let your faith in the Lord guide you to those who are prepared to receive the gospel of Jesus Christ.

I have often taught that one of the ways you can be involved in sharing the gospel is to write down a date in the next two or three months that you want to have someone prepared to be taught by the missionaries. Then ask your Father in Heaven for guidance and help. Ask Him to bless you to be alert and prepared.

May I feel a great pleasure and joy in doing my part, and a greater pleasure and joy in seeing all the Latter-day Saints doing their part towards carrying this grand gospel to all the nations of the earth, that they may hear and, if it please God, yield obedience to the truth.
—Hyrum Mack Smith

Let me share with you a couple of experiences members have had in doing this. Sometime after I talked about this concept in general conference, I received from a woman a letter that was quite startling in content. It said, "Dear Brother Ballard. I hate to tell you this but you are a false prophet. I did what you told us to do, and we had no success. Therefore you should not be teaching the people to do this." She really got after me. It was not a gentle letter.

Well, I read it, and I have learned when I receive a letter like that not to answer it for a couple of days so I can think it through a little better. The thought came to me: "I am not going to answer the letter in writing; I am going to call her on the telephone and talk to her." So I tracked her down and got her on the phone. I said, "This is Elder Ballard." And she said, "Who?" I said, "This is Elder Ballard of the Quorum of the Twelve Apostles. I am calling you about your letter." There was dead silence for a moment. I said, "I am calling to apologize to you. I am terribly sorry that you have had such unfortunate circumstances in attempting to do missionary work by setting a date. I am asking you if you will forgive me."

She said, "Oh, Brother Ballard, you didn't need to call me. I just wanted to bring to your attention that it didn't work."

I said, "Will you forgive me?"

She said, "Oh, certainly."

I said, "Would you also be kind enough to answer one question?" She responded that she would if she could.

"Will you tell me whom you talked to during the time that you were fasting and praying to find somebody for the missionaries to teach?"

Dead silence.

I asked, "Are you still there?"

"Yes, I am."

I said, "Will you tell me?"

She said, "Well, to be honest with you, we didn't do that."

"In other words, what you thought I said was all you had to do was pray and fast and then in some miraculous way you would have someone for the missionaries to teach?"

Calling her by name, I said, "Would you set another date, only this time will you talk to the people in the grocery store, at the service station, in the beauty parlor? Everywhere you go, will you open your mouth and let the Lord help you be successful with this effort?" She was a good sport and said she would.

It was less than a month later that I received another letter telling me that the missionaries were teaching a family in their home that she had met at the grocery store.

> *May the Lord speed that glorious day, and continue to send His message forward by the faithful, devoted help of the members of the Church, so that no soul may be ignorant of the dangers that are before us, or be denied the privilege of that protection and safety which the Lord has offered to all His children.*
>
> —Melvin J. Ballard

I taught that concept in a stake conference, and everybody was excited. They were going to do it. Then, about six months later, I got a letter from the wonderful stake president in whose home I had stayed in that area. Here is what his letter said:

"Dear Elder Ballard, your words have been haunting me for six months. I have known I should set a date with my family, but we hadn't done it. Then we finally did. A month ago we set a date. When we did that we started to pray. The first fast Sunday, we fasted with that as our purpose. I want to tell you what happened."

This stake president was an attorney. The very week that they set a date as a family, a young couple came to his law office. They had been referred to him as one who would treat them well and be honest and fair with them in helping them finalize their divorce.

The letter continued: "I looked at that couple and said something I never ever dreamed I would ever say to a potential client: 'You don't need a divorce. What you need is the gospel of Jesus Christ. Now, what I would like you to do is let me teach you about the restoration of the gospel of Jesus Christ. If when we conclude you have not resolved to stay together and make your marriage a success, then I will handle your divorce and not charge you a penny.'"

He and his family had been on their knees praying for guidance, and the Spirit prompted him about what to say to the couple.

Well, after the missionaries taught them the gospel, they were baptized. They found the greatest thing in their life the day they walked into the stake president's law office.

Fourth, we should strive to save the souls of those who have departed this life without obtaining a knowledge of Jesus Christ and the sacred ordinances of His gospel. We do this by identifying our kindred dead and by performing the ordinances for them in the holy temples. During the Orlando Temple open house, I spoke with a priest from another faith as he was leaving the temple. With great emotion, he expressed that there are only two times he had really felt a strong spirit of the Lord. The first was at the garden tomb, and the second was in the celestial room of our temple. Our temples are sacred, and the work performed there is truly the work of saving souls.

Every child of God will have the opportunity to hear and accept the saving ordinances of the gospel of Jesus Christ either in this life or in the spirit world. President Joseph F. Smith revealed this truth:

> I beheld that the faithful elders of this dispensation, when they depart from mortal life, continue their labors in the preaching of the gospel of repentance and redemption, through the sacrifice of the Only Begotten Son of God, among those who are in darkness and under the bondage of sin in the great world of the spirits of the dead.
>
> The dead who repent will be redeemed, through obedience to the ordinances of the house of God.
>
> And after they have paid the penalty of their transgressions, and are washed clean, shall receive a reward according to their works, for they are heirs of salvation.
>
> Thus was the vision of the redemption of the dead revealed to me, and I bear record, and I know that this record is true, through the blessing of our Lord and Savior, Jesus Christ (Doctrine and Covenants 138:57–60).

How beautiful and consistent it is that the Lord would give to those . . . who died when truth was not upon the earth, the same privilege He gives to those who reach maturity and who enjoy the opportunities, the power and the blessed privileges of the gospel.
—MELVIN J. BALLARD

What a blessing is ours to understand the great plan of happiness our Heavenly Father has revealed to us through His prophets! Our opportunity to help save the souls of the living and the dead is, of course, made possible through the Atonement of the

Lord Jesus Christ. Through His love and mercy, Christ became our Redeemer by suffering for the sins of all mankind in the Garden of Gethsemane and on the cross at Golgotha. In so doing, Jesus provided a way for us to repent and overcome the temptations of the world. Through His Resurrection and our blessing to follow Him, we can return to the presence of our Heavenly Father. Again I repeat, the Savior made it simple and clear: "If ye love me, keep my commandments" (John 14:15).

I fear some of us have not caught the vision of the magnitude of the work this Church is expected to perform, not only for its members but also for the world, for we have a world mission, and world problems can be solved by this Church.
—Melvin J. Ballard

For all of Heavenly Father's children to receive the full blessings of the Savior's Atonement, those of us who have received the knowledge of the eternal plan of salvation are expected to do all we can in helping others receive the same. We need to be in a hurry to share these blessings with our immediate and extended family members, our neighbors, our associates, and those we come in contact with in our many activities of life.

Now, after all is said and done, we are individually accountable for the salvation of our own souls. We alone can accept the Savior's invitation to come unto Him—to accept His Atonement in our lives by increasing our faith in Him, repenting, being baptized, and partaking of the sacrament to renew our baptismal promises. We cannot sidestep this reality. Each one of us needs to repent, strive to live righteously, receive all the ordinances of the gospel, and faithfully keep our covenants. The Lord has promised that our work to bring Heavenly Father's precious children to Him is a way to show our love and also a way to receive forgiveness for our own sins (see Doctrine and Covenants 62:3).

May we all drive the roots of our testimony of Jesus Christ and His restored gospel deep into our hearts so that the winds of evil, adversity, and temptation and the cares of the world will not uproot our faith. And may we always do our part in helping to find and teach the precious children of our Heavenly Father. I know if we will try a little harder, pray a little more fervently, and care a little more for others of our Father in Heaven's children, He will bless us with an increased spiritual knowledge and power to bring many more of His children the joy and blessings of the gospel of Jesus Christ.

> *We want knowledge and wisdom. We want to understand the truth, and understanding the truth rejoice in it. We want to know what the commandments of God are, and knowing them we are determined, as a people, to keep them, that we might come to a knowledge of all truth.*
> —Hyrum Mack Smith

May the peace of the Lord be in your home. May it be in your heart. May you be stirred with a great desire to reach out and strengthen the wards, the branches, the stakes, and the temples, that the work of the Lord will continue to shine and move forward more rapidly.

CHAPTER 5

Building Bridges of Understanding

MANY YEARS AGO, I tried my hand for the first time at writing a book. For years I had felt the need for a book about the Church that would explain in simple terms our beliefs and our doctrinal position in relationship to all other churches. My attempt resulted in the publication of *Our Search for Happiness.* The one question I kept asking myself was, "What is it that I want to have happen with anyone who might read the book?" The word *understanding* kept coming into my mind. Let me share a few words from that book:

> *A new day has dawned for the Church, a day of understanding and a day of demonstration. This day comes at a time when the world needs the very things that the Church is undertaking to accomplish as an example to them.*
> —MELVIN J. BALLARD

"Consider for a moment the word *understanding.*

"It's a simple word, really—one that most of us use every day. But it means something that is quite remarkable. With understanding we can strengthen relationships, revitalize neighborhoods, unify nations, and even bring peace to a troubled world. Without it chaos, intolerance, hate, and war are often the result.

"In other words, *mis*understanding."

I went on to cite the eleventh Article of Faith: "We claim the privilege of worshiping Almighty God according to the dictates of our own conscience, and allow all men the same privilege, let them worship how, where, or what they may" (Articles of Faith 1:11).

"We really do believe that," I wrote. "Just as we claim the right to worship as we choose, we believe [others] have the right to worship—or to not worship—as [they] see fit. All of our interpersonal relationships should be built on a foundation of mutual respect, trust, and appreciation. But that shouldn't prevent us from sharing deeply held religious feelings with each other. Indeed, we may find that our [religious and] philosophical differences add flavor and perspective to our relationships, especially if those relationships are built on true values, openness, respect, trust, and understanding. *Especially* understanding" (*Our Search for Happiness,* 1, 5).

> *We should go forth . . . with the sole desire in our hearts to manifest unto them that which God has revealed unto us, and carry to them that which has made us free and happy.*
> —Hyrum Mack Smith

Each one of us needs to know that the gospel of Jesus Christ has been restored to the earth through the Prophet Joseph Smith. Priesthood authority is once again upon the earth so that sacred ordinances may be performed for the eternal blessing of all those who will accept the fulness of the gospel of Jesus Christ and all that it has to offer. Significant eternal truths have been restored, and they are the very foundation of our faith. Yet not only do we need to know and understand these true doctrines for ourselves, but also there is a great need for us as members of the Church to know how to courteously share our testimonies and beliefs with others while maintaining their friendship and goodwill.

Although we as Latter-day Saints are pleased to share the good news of the restored gospel of Jesus Christ with any and all who will hear our message, sometimes the only thing we can accomplish with our friends is to help them understand our basic beliefs.

We must remember that the Lord expects us to peacefully coexist with others not of our faith (see Articles of Faith 1:11). We can pleasantly agree to disagree with them on certain points of doctrine even while we unite with them in the great common denominators of faith in God and benevolent service to others.

> *We invite . . . all to come and talk with us and reason with us as sensible and reasonable men [and women]. Come in a friendly spirit and if you cannot be convinced, go in a friendly spirit. You will be received in a friendly spirit and dismissed in friendliness, whichever way it results.*
> —Hyrum Mack Smith

As members of the Church, we need to be kind and gentle in our conversations as we express our convictions and feelings that the gospel of Jesus Christ has been restored to the earth in its fulness through the Prophet Joseph Smith. As appropriate, we need to teach and testify and discern when it might be helpful to give the Book of Mormon and other Church literature to those who show interest.

When we are guided by the Spirit, I find that our conversations will often lead to the subject of the Fatherhood of God and the brotherhood of man. All of us, regardless of race, color, or creed, belong to the family of our Heavenly Father. Our understanding and knowledge of this basic truth should compel us to love all our brothers and sisters and to share the eternal plan of salvation with them. To those who are interested, it might be well to explain our belief that the brotherhood of man includes our teaching that we all existed premortally as spirit children of God, our Heavenly Father, where we learned and accepted His plan for us to come to earth to gain a mortal body and be tested. Our deep-rooted respect for all mankind is enhanced by our understanding of our premortal life and experiences together.

With this as background, let me discuss with you five subjects that I often find lend themselves to misunderstanding when we share our doctrinal position with others. Some claim we are not Christians because of our belief in these revealed truths.

ADDITIONAL BOOKS OF SCRIPTURE

The first concerns our acceptance of other books of scripture beside the books contained in the Bible. These books, of course, are the Book of Mormon, the Doctrine and Covenants, and the Pearl of Great Price. To others who question the need for these scriptures, we can explain that the bedrock doctrines of the restored Church are based on revelation to a modern prophet of God. We believe that God raised up a prophet in our time, even Joseph Smith, and gave to him revelations, authority, and commandments as they pertain to our day.

The great pronouncement of the Lord at the beginning of this dispensation is contained in section 1 of the Doctrine and Covenants:

> Wherefore, I the Lord, knowing the calamity which should come upon the inhabitants of the earth, called upon my servant Joseph Smith, Jun., and spake unto him from heaven, and gave him commandments;
>
> And also gave commandments to others, that they should proclaim these things unto the world; and all this that it might be fulfilled, which was written by the prophets— . . .
>
> And also those to whom these commandments were given, might have power to lay the foundation of this church, and to bring it forth out of obscurity and out of darkness, the only true and living church

The Book of Mormon is indeed from God. . . . Does it not contain revelations and visions similar to the Bible? Does it not contain the same glorious gospel, and the same mighty exhortations to men to serve God and to turn from their evil ways? Yes. . . . They are the pure words of God, as they were given through the inspiration of the Spirit to the prophets who wrote them anciently.
—Hyrum Mack Smith

upon the face of the whole earth (Doctrine and Covenants 1:17–18, 30).

Now, those words from the Lord are either true or they are not. Either Joseph Smith is the Lord's instrument by which the Restoration of the gospel of Jesus Christ in its fulness was accomplished, or he is not. There is no possible compromise of this point. Yet, even when we are bearing testimony of these truths, we must be cordial in the way we express and explain them.

The message we share with all mankind is that The Church of Jesus Christ of Latter-day Saints is the same as the church Jesus Christ established during His mortal ministry, restored in its fulness in these latter days. This truth is based on the fact that God the Father and His Beloved Son, Jesus Christ, have spoken to a modern-day prophet and have revealed themselves anew to the world. The keys and priesthood authority given to Joseph Smith to establish the Church of Jesus Christ upon the earth have come down to our current prophet. All the laws, covenants, and ordinances of the gospel and the priesthood authority by which men and women can receive the ordinances of salvation have been restored.

We do not claim Joseph Smith was a perfect man; neither do the Latter-day Saints worship him. We love him because he loved his fellow men and because he gave his life to establish the doctrines which we hold as sacred and true. And so we love him, perhaps, as much as a mortal man ever was loved by a people, but we do not worship him.
—Melvin J. Ballard

Thus, we can say to our friends, "Yes, without question, we believe in revelation and scripture in addition to that contained within the Holy Bible." We can kindly explain that although we accept the Bible as the word of God as far as it is translated correctly, we believe that this generation has as much, if not more, of a need for God's guidance and direction than generations of former times. Our belief that our Heavenly Father has sent prophets and apostles and has given us additional scripture for our day and time is a manifestation of His great love and concern for His children. If someone chooses not to accept our beliefs, then we should kindly agree to disagree, while encouraging understanding.

> *You Latter-day Saints ought to praise God; but in your thankfulness for the greater blessings which you enjoy, you ought not to denounce others because they have not so much good as you have.*
>
> —Hyrum Mack Smith

OUR UNDERSTANDING OF GRACE

A second reason why some people think Latter-day Saints are not Christian is their belief that we do not accept the doctrine of salvation through the grace of our Lord Jesus Christ. Wise are the members of the Church who can visit with those who have this misunderstanding and in kind and factual ways build bridges of understanding by teaching that we accept the doctrine of salvation through the grace of God and His Beloved Son, the Lord Jesus Christ.

We believe our Father in Heaven is a God of love and mercy. He is desirous that all of us have joy and eternal happiness. Therefore, before our world was created, He provided an eternal plan for our salvation. The Book of Mormon calls it the "plan of happiness" (Alma 42:16).

Our Heavenly Father's loving grace or goodness is demonstrated in part by the creation of this beautiful earth with all its bounties. To each of us He has given the precious gift of agency, through which we choose between pathways that lead to happiness or ones that lead to misery (see 2 Nephi 2:27). With perfect foreknowledge, our Heavenly Father knew what His children would experience as a result of the Fall of Adam. Each of us would be subjected to the conditions of temptation, sin, bodily infirmities, and physical death.

The majority of our Father's children are in ignorance concerning the resurrection which affects every human being who ever has lived or who ever shall live in the earth. To those who believed, what joy was in their hearts.
—Melvin J. Ballard

Heavenly Father loved us so much that He sent to this earth His Beloved Son, Jesus Christ, as our Savior and Redeemer (see John 3:16–17). I mention only two of the many things that Jesus accomplished for us that we could not do for ourselves. First, at the conclusion of His mortal ministry, He suffered the Atonement, through which He took upon Himself all our sins and infirmities, suffering "these things for all, that [we] might not suffer if [we] would repent" (Doctrine and Covenants 19:16). And second, He broke the bands of death and made it possible for all mankind to be resurrected. This means that after our physical death, we will gain a resurrected, physical body.

If we exercise faith in Him, repent, and are faithful to the gospel covenants we make in the ordinances of salvation, our bodies will be glorified like the sun (see 1 Corinthians 15:40–41). I want to emphasize strongly that all of this is made possible through the grace of Jesus Christ. That is why the great Book of Mormon prophet Nephi wrote, "And we talk of Christ, we rejoice in Christ, we preach of Christ, we prophesy of Christ, and we write according to our prophecies, that our children may know to what source they may look for a remission of their sins" (2 Nephi 25:26).

In the Christian world, there has been much debate regarding the relationship of grace and works. To The Church of Jesus Christ of Latter-day Saints, both are core doctrines. Just as a pair of scissors requires two blades to function, the Lord's grace and our works of faith in Christ, personal repentance, and receiving saving ordinances are required for eternal life in God's presence.

Our works consist of placing our full confidence and trust in Jesus Christ and then exercising our desire and willingness to live by His teachings. We do this by repenting of all our sins and obeying the laws and ordinances of Christ's gospel. As we do this faithfully over our lifetime, we are sanctified by the Holy Ghost, and our nature is changed.

The scriptures inform us that Jesus grew from "grace to grace" until He received a fulness of the Father's grace (Doctrine and Covenants 93:13). What I understand that to mean is that He obeyed His Heavenly Father's will and by so doing received an increase of our Heavenly Father's power. Thus, He increased in the divine attributes of godliness until He was perfect in virtue and holiness like His Father. Jesus thereby showed us the path of holiness and then promised us: "If you keep my commandments, you shall receive of his fulness, and be glorified in me as I am in the Father; therefore, I say unto you, you shall receive grace for grace" (Doctrine and Covenants 93:20).

> *We believe that among all professed Christians, a community that puts into practice the word of God, . . . that enjoys the blessings promised by obedience to the commandments of the Lord, [produces] men and women who are more virtuous, more honest, more faithful, more prayerful, and more honorable than any other community. . . . We are willing now, and at any time, as I say, to be judged by our fruits.*
> —HYRUM MACK SMITH

The doctrine of The Church of Jesus Christ of Latter-day Saints regarding grace is forthright. We understand that because we have all become spiritually unclean as a result of sin (see 1 John 1:8) and because "there cannot any unclean thing enter into the kingdom of God" (1 Nephi 15:34), no individual can receive eternal life solely on the merits of his or her own effort. We believe that only as we rely on the

Savior's grace and demonstrate our changed nature through obedience to His laws and ordinances may we receive eternal life. This principle is beautifully taught by Moroni in the closing chapter of the Book of Mormon. Please note the harmony and balance between the efforts we must make and the role of God's grace in the process of perfecting ourselves.

> Yea, come unto Christ, and be perfected in him, and deny yourselves of all ungodliness; and if ye shall deny yourselves of all ungodliness, and love God with all your might, mind and strength, then is his grace sufficient for you, that by his grace ye may be perfect in Christ; and if by the grace of God ye are perfect in Christ, ye can in nowise deny the power of God.
>
> And again, if ye by the grace of God are perfect in Christ, and deny not his power, then are ye sanctified in Christ by the grace of God, through the shedding of the blood of Christ, which is in the covenant of the Father unto the remission of your sins, that ye become holy, without spot. (Moroni 10:32–33)

Let us thank [God] with all our hearts for His Beloved Son, Jesus Christ, who loved [us] so that He died for [us], and who hath purchased us and hath redeemed us.
—Melvin J. Ballard

We believe that this should be the goal each of us is striving for.

It is only through the infinite Atonement of Jesus Christ that people can overcome the consequences of bad choices. Thus, Nephi teaches us that it is ultimately by the grace of Christ that we are saved even after all that we can do (see 2 Nephi 25:23). No matter how hard we work, no matter how much we obey, no matter how many good things we do in this life, it would not be enough were it not for Jesus Christ and His loving grace. On our own, we cannot earn the kingdom of God—no matter what we do. Unfortunately, there are some within the Church who have become so preoccupied with performing good works that they forget that those works—as good as they may be—are hollow unless they are accompanied by a complete dependence on Christ. It is this dependence that causes us to want to sing what Alma eloquently referred to as "the song of redeeming love" (Alma 5:26).

> *The very image of God is impressed upon the children of men. They belong to Him; He owns them, and He will never rest until He has brought them into a condition where they gladly and voluntarily render unto God that which belongs to God.*
>
> —Hyrum Mack Smith

You remember that quote from the fifth chapter of Alma, in the Book of Mormon, in which he asks a series of powerful questions that are instructive in this matter. He asked members of the church at that time:

> Have ye spiritually been born of God? Have ye received his image in your countenances? Have ye experienced this mighty change in your hearts?
>
> Do ye exercise faith in the redemption of him who created you? Do you look forward with an eye of faith, and view this mortal body raised in immortality, and this corruption raised in incorruption, to stand before God to be judged according to the deeds which have been done in the mortal body? . . .
>
> Or do ye imagine to yourselves that ye can lie unto the Lord in that day, and say—Lord, our works have been righteous works upon the face of the earth—and that he will save you? . . .
>
> I say unto you, can ye look up to God at that day with a pure heart and clean hands? I say unto you, can you look up, having the image of God engraven upon your countenances? . . .
>
> I say unto you, ye will know at that day that ye cannot be saved; for there can no man be saved except his garments

> are washed white; yea, his garments must be purified until they are cleansed from all stain, through the blood of him of whom it has been spoken by our fathers, who should come to redeem his people from their sins. . . .
>
> And now behold, I say unto you, my brethren, if ye have experienced a change of heart, and if ye have felt to sing the song of redeeming love, I would ask, can ye feel so now? . . .
>
> Behold, he sendeth an invitation unto all men, for the arms of mercy are extended towards them, and he saith: Repent, and I will receive you. (Alma 5:14–15, 17, 19, 21, 26, 33)

All has been given us that we are capable of receiving. And Oh! How we rejoice in it, my brethren and sisters, and in the knowledge, too, that eye hath not seen, nor ear heard, neither hath it entered into our hearts, what God has in store for us as we march on in that infinite progression and advancement. All things will be given to us—all power, all glory, all knowledge, even as our Father in Heaven possesses it—in due time, as we are capable of receiving them.

—Hyrum Mack Smith

Let us never forget that it is by and through the grace of Jesus Christ and our coming unto Him through spiritual rebirth that the happy possibilities of eternal life are available to all of us.

A great demonstration of the love, mercy, and grace of our Heavenly Father is His preparing kingdoms of glory for His children's eventual eternal residence based on the exercise of our personal agency relative to the commandments of God. Even the telestial glory surpasses our understanding. If we obey the laws of the gospel, we will receive a celestial glory. In other words, the Lord has said that we will be rewarded on the basis of "that which [we] are willing to receive" (Doctrine and Covenants 88:32). Remember, the Apostle Paul compares the difference between these two kingdoms as the difference between the brightness of the sun and that of the stars (see 1 Corinthians 15:40–41).

OUR RELATIONSHIP WITH CHRIST

A third area of misunderstanding that I'd like to discuss has to do with our relationship to Christ. We occasionally hear some members refer to Jesus as our Elder Brother, which is a true concept based on our understanding of the premortal life with our Father in Heaven. But like many points of gospel doctrine, that simple truth doesn't go far enough in terms of describing the Savior's role in our present lives and His great position as a member of the Godhead. Thus, some non-LDS Christians are uncomfortable with what they perceive as a secondary role for Christ in our theology. They feel that we view Jesus as a spiritual peer. They believe that we view Christ as an implementer for God, if you will, but that we don't view Him as God to us and to all mankind, which, of course, is counter to biblical testimony about Christ's divinity.

We will continue to testify that Jesus Christ is the Redeemer of the world; that He died for the sins of mankind; that He came forth from the Father, begotten of God and born of woman; that He grew to manhood; that He preached the gospel of salvation, and was crucified, after which he went into the spirit world and there proclaimed liberty to the captive, and opened the prison doors to them that were bound.
—Hyrum Mack Smith

Let me help us understand, with clarity and testimony, our belief about Jesus Christ. We declare He is the King of kings, Lord of lords, the Creator, the Savior, the Captain of our Salvation, the Bright and Morning Star. He has taught us that He is in all things, above all things, through all things, and round about all things, that He is Alpha and Omega, the Lord of the Universe, the first and the last relative to our salvation. His name is above every name and is, in fact, the only name under heaven by which we can be saved (see Bible Dictionary, s.v. "Christ").

Further, the Lord Himself, as recorded in the Book of Mormon, told the brother of

Jared, "Behold, I am Jesus Christ. I am the Father and the Son. In me shall all mankind have life, and that eternally, even they who shall believe on my name; and they shall become my sons and my daughters" (Ether 3:14).

> *This conception of the Latter-day Saints, that Jesus Christ was verily the Son of God, . . . becomes essential in order to qualify Him to fulfill His great mission. Why did He come to earth? He had glory enough. He was a God and had produced worlds; he stood in honor; but He had a sacred mission to perform upon earth. He came to atone for the fall of man. . . . The death of every man that had descended from Adam could not pay the price; it required someone with just the qualities in him that Jesus Christ had.*
> —Melvin J. Ballard

But how is that possible? How can Jesus Christ be both the Father and the Son? It really isn't as complicated as it sounds. Though He is the Son of God, He is the head of the Church, which is the family of believers. When we are spiritually born again, we are adopted into His family. He becomes our Father or leader. To further explain this concept of Jesus also being our "Father," let me use an analogy and say that seven of my premortal spirit brothers and sisters were born to my wife, Barbara, and me. We are therefore their premortal spiritual brother and sister and also their earthly, physical father and mother. Similarly, Christ is our spiritual Elder Brother and the Son of God, but He is also our Father or leader and our God. King Benjamin taught his faithful followers that "because of the covenant which ye have made [through the baptism of fire or spiritual rebirth] ye shall be called the children of Christ, his sons, and his daughters; for behold, this day he hath spiritually begotten you; for ye say that your hearts are changed through faith on his name; therefore, ye are born of him and have become his sons and his daughters" (Mosiah 5:7).

In no way does this doctrine denigrate the role of God the

Father. Rather, we believe it enhances our understanding of the role of God the Son, our Savior, Jesus Christ. God our Heavenly Father is the Father of our spirits; we speak of God the Son as the Father of the righteous. He is regarded as the "Father" because of the relationship between Him and those who accept His gospel, thereby becoming heirs of eternal life. And the third member of the Godhead, God the Holy Ghost, has the specific mission to teach and to testify of truth as it pertains to the divinity of both God the Father and God the Son.

Now, we can understand why some Latter-day Saints have tended to focus on Christ's Sonship as opposed to His Godhood. As members of earthly families, we can relate to Him as a child, as a Son, and as a brother because we know how that feels. We can personalize that relationship because we ourselves are children, sons and daughters, brothers and sisters. For some it may be more difficult to relate to Him as a God. And so in an attempt to draw closer to Christ and to cultivate warm and personal feelings toward Him, some tend to humanize Him, sometimes at the expense of acknowledging His divinity. So let us be very clear on this point: it is true that Jesus was our Elder Brother in the premortal life, but we believe that in this life it is crucial that we become "born again" as His sons and daughters in the gospel covenant.

> *This wonderful Friend has indeed purchased us, and He came to earth to do it; He came to pay the price, and He holds the key and shall unlock the door for the exaltation and the salvation, according to man's will and desire, . . . to bring us to glory, to immortality and eternal life. That is God's gift to the world—this precious Son.*
> —Melvin J. Ballard

With this background, we need to understand that there are many in the Christian world who believe this doctrine is inappropriate. In fact, there are many who say that Latter-day Saints believe in a "different Jesus" than do other Christians and that we therefore are not "Christian." Here is another place that we can agree to disagree without being disagreeable. We believe in the Jesus of the New Testament, and we believe what the New Testament teaches about Him. We do believe things about Jesus that other Christians do not believe, but that is because we know, through revelation, things about Jesus that others do not know. It is a twisting of language to call this a "different Jesus," as though we have created some other individual by that name.

OUR BELIEF ABOUT THE GODHEAD

During the few moments that Joseph Smith stood in the presence of the Father and the Son in the Sacred Grove, he learned more about the Father and about His Son Jesus Christ than all the philosophers and professors of religion of all the ages ever have known, or ever will know, unless they shall have a like privilege and opportunity. So we speak with positiveness upon these subjects, and yet we hope with tolerance; but we know whereof we speak, that we do declare the truth.

—Melvin J. Ballard

A fourth area of misunderstanding among some of our friends in Christianity is that they refer to us as "polytheists," meaning that we believe in a plurality of Gods. Much misunderstanding would be avoided if they understood that we worship only one Godhead, consisting of God the Father, God the Son, and God the Holy Ghost. We believe that the biblical record teaches that God the Father, Jesus Christ, and the Holy Ghost are separate persons. When the Savior was baptized, the Father spoke His approval from heaven, and the Holy Ghost was witnessed to be present by the sign of a dove (see Matthew 3:16–17). Likewise, the Bible records the prayers of Jesus Christ to our Father in Heaven, a separate being (see John 17:3). We believe this doctrine is taught in the Bible despite what the creeds of other Christian denominations may teach. Such creeds were created hundreds of years after Christ's mortal ministry through the processes of debate and compromise, often at the expense of biblical truths. The falling away from the teachings of Jesus Christ resulted in the Apostasy, which made the Restoration of the gospel essential. This is a subject to be studied by all; the various Christian creeds were born through church councils and other efforts to define the true nature of God and His Son, Jesus Christ. Through revelations to modern prophets, we now know God the Father, God the Son, and God the Holy Ghost and our true relationship to each one of them.

There is another related dimension of the scriptures that causes discomfort for many traditional Christians regarding this whole matter. We believe our Father in Heaven has promised His faithful sons and daughters "all things"—even that those worthy of exaltation in the celestial kingdom will be as "gods, even the sons of God" and that "these shall dwell in the presence of God and His Christ forever and ever" (see Doctrine and Covenants 76:55, 58, 62). Although we do not know the full detail of these promises or what is fully meant by being "gods, even the sons of God," we do accept these promises as revealed doctrine. Yet notwithstanding these promises, we say that for us, there is indeed no other object of worship than God the Father, the Son, and the Holy Ghost.

THE NATURE OF GOD

The final area of misunderstanding that I want to address has to do with our belief that "the Father has a body of flesh and bones as tangible as man's; the Son also" (Doctrine and Covenants 130:22). As Latter-day Saints, we believe that the resurrected Christ has a body of flesh and bones (see Luke 24:39). Now, if Jesus is the express image of God the Father, which we believe that He is, then God the Father has a body of flesh and bones as tangible as man's. Most Christians who accept the Bible believe that Christ will come again and will even show the wounds in His hands. As one ancient prophet has declared, he will show those wounds to others and say they are "those with which I was wounded in the house of my friends" (Zechariah 13:6). We believe that Jesus did not and in the future will not discard His resurrected body. God the Father and His Only Begotten Son, Jesus Christ, are glorified, exalted beings, and from the moment of the appearance of the Father and the Son to Joseph Smith, we have known their true nature.

May I suggest that what we want most of all is for Christian and non-Christian alike to understand that we love the Lord Jesus Christ. We revere His name. We count it a great honor and privilege to take upon ourselves the name of Christ as Christians and as members of The Church of Jesus Christ of Latter-day Saints. Yet, although "we claim the privilege of worshiping Almighty God according to the dictates of our own conscience," we "allow all men the same privilege, let them worship how, where, or what they may" (Articles of Faith 1:11). Further, just because people of other faiths don't believe everything that we believe about Jesus Christ and His eternal ministry, we don't deny that they are Christian. They are simply different from us in some of their beliefs. Although we may differ in points of doctrine, and although we may wish to share with them marvelous truths that we believe the Lord Himself has revealed in these last days, we will and must respect their Christianity and ask only that they likewise respect ours.

> *We wish our friends would be a little more sensible, a little more reasonable, and a little more charitable, exercising towards their fellow men who do not see as they see, a little more of the spirit of brotherly kindness and toleration.*
> —Hyrum Mack Smith

There are other areas where misunderstandings may occur; it is not possible to list all of them. My intent in sharing these concepts is to encourage you to become a lifelong student of the scriptures and the restored gospel of Jesus Christ so that you might always be prepared to courteously and respectfully help clarify misunderstandings about our Church as they occur with those of other faiths. Notwithstanding our efforts to build bridges of understanding and to be charitable in all our dealings, we have the same obligation the Savior issued to Peter: "When thou art converted, strengthen thy brethren" (Luke 22:32). When opportunities present themselves to you in the course of your life, may the Lord bless you to share the gospel generously and kindly with your family, your friends, your work associates, and any others who are not members of the Church to bring about a better understanding of the Restoration of the gospel. That is our responsibility as Christians. That is the responsibility of every member of The Church of Jesus Christ of Latter-day Saints.

CHAPTER 6

Here Am I, Send Me

I have been married to Sister Ballard for more than sixty years. The greatest day in my life was the day I met her. My greatest accomplishment was convincing her I was the only true and living returned missionary among all of those that she was dating. It was a most important day when we were married in the Salt Lake Temple. We are the parents of two sons and five daughters. Perhaps being the father of our five daughters, the grandfather of twenty-four granddaughters, and great grandfather of twenty-two and counting great-granddaughters has given me some insight and experience about the lives, accomplishments, and contributions of women in the Church and in our families.

Initially, I intended to address these thoughts specifically to women. But as I have considered the days that lie ahead, I believe this message is vital to both men and women. So I invite men to pay strict attention as well. Please remember that it was the Lord who said, after addressing Emma Smith, "And verily, verily, I say unto you, that this is my voice unto all" (Doctrine and Covenants 25:16). Apparently, there are general principles anyone, including men, can gain by listening to the Lord's counsel given to a woman.

Dear brethren, your lives have and will be influenced by your mothers, sisters, wives, daughters, and those women with whom you will be privileged to serve and labor in the Church, in the community, and at your work.

Let me set the stage by sharing a letter sent to Church

headquarters. This woman wrote: "I have a wonderful husband and children, whom I love deeply. I love the Lord and His Church more than I can say. I know the Church is true! I realize I shouldn't feel discouraged about who I am. Yet I have been going through an identity crisis most of my life. I have never dared utter these feelings out loud but have hidden them behind the huge, confident smile I wear to church every week. For years I have doubted if I had any value beyond my roles as a wife and mother. I have feared that men are that they might have joy, but that women are that they might be overlooked. I long to feel that I as a woman matter to the Lord."

I would like to respond to the issue that underlies the concern of this faithful woman. Does the Lord respect women? Do women matter to the Lord? Yes. The answer is a resounding yes!

Elder James E. Talmage stated that "the world's greatest champion of woman and womanhood is Jesus Christ" (*Jesus the Christ,* 475). I believe that is a true statement.

The New Testament Gospels reveal how Jesus interacted with women in ways first-century women and men may not have expected. According to the Gospel of John, the first time the Lord acknowledged Himself to be the Messiah (Christ) was to a Samaritan woman at Jacob's well. He taught her about living water and proclaimed, simply, "I . . . am he" (John 4:26). And it was Martha to whom He proclaimed: "I am the resurrection, and the life. . . . And whosoever liveth and believeth in me shall never die" (John 11:25–26).

> *Our Father in Heaven does not stand alone; for side by side with Him, in all her glory, a glory like unto His, stands a companion. . . . For as we have a Father in heaven, so also we have a Mother there, a glorified, exalted, ennobled Mother.*
>
> —MELVIN J. BALLARD

And then, during His greatest agony as He hung on the cross, the Savior reached out to one person—His mother—when in that terrible but glorious moment He finished His work among God's children. In compassion, love, devotion, and honor, the suffering, atoning, and dying Savior asked John the Beloved to care for her as though she were his own mother (see John 19:26–27).

> *Search from the highest forms of life to the lowest and most insignificant, and I defy any man to find a living creature without a mother. If that is true, then there are no creatures that live that have not had mothers. . . . You don't suppose that woman is going to be annihilated when death ends mortality. She is going to live just as well as man will live, forever and ever. But she will live a woman. There are no heights to which man shall aspire and attain in which woman shall not be, side by side, with him.*
>
> —Melvin J. Ballard

Of this you may be certain: The Lord especially loves righteous women—women who are not only faithful but filled with faith, women who are optimistic and cheerful because they know who they are and where they are going, women who are striving to live and serve as women of God.

There are those who suggest that males are favored of the Lord because they are ordained to hold the priesthood. Anyone who believes that does not understand the great plan of happiness. The premortal and mortal natures of men and women were specified by the Lord Jehovah Himself, and it is simply not within His divine character to diminish the roles and responsibilities of any of His children.

As President Joseph Fielding Smith explained, "The Lord offers to his daughters every spiritual gift and blessing that can be obtained by his sons" (*Improvement Era,* June 1970, 66). All of us, men and women alike, are accepted of the Lord based on the same standard, "All those who receive my gospel are sons and daughters in my kingdom" (Doctrine and Covenants 25:1). Specifically, we can become "the children of Christ, his sons, and his daughters," through faith on the name of Jesus Christ (Mosiah 5:7).

We each receive the gift of the Holy Ghost and are entitled to personal revelation (see Doctrine and Covenants 25:8). We may *all* take upon us the Lord's name (Doctrine and Covenants 18:21–23). We each partake of the sacrament each week, renewing the same covenants. We also receive the ordinances of the temple from which we emerge endowed with power without distinction based on race, ethnicity, or gender. We each are promised the blessings of exaltation and eternal lives through the same covenants made in the house of the Lord (see Doctrine and Covenants 76:50–54).

President Joseph Fielding Smith stated, "It is within the privilege of sisters of this Church to receive exaltation in the kingdom of God and receive authority and power as queens and priestesses" (as quoted in *Daughters in My Kingdom*, 133).

Let it be understood that all spiritual blessings given by God are available to men and women alike according to their faithfulness and their desire to receive them. Nephi taught, "He inviteth them all to come unto him and partake of his goodness; and he denieth none that come unto him, black and white, bond and free, *male and female*" (2 Nephi 26:33; emphasis added).

The basic doctrinal purpose for the creation of the earth is to provide for God's spirit children the continuation of the process of exaltation and eternal life. God said to Moses, "And I, God, created man in mine own image, in the image of mine Only Begotten created I him; male and female created I them. And I, God, blessed them, and said unto them: Be fruitful, and multiply, and replenish the earth" (Moses 2:27–28).

"The Family: A Proclamation to the World" confirms that God has neither revoked nor changed this commandment. The First Presidency and the Twelve Apostles "solemnly proclaim that marriage between a man and a woman is ordained of God and that the family is central to the Creator's plan for the eternal destiny of His children."

This doctrine sometimes causes women to ask: "Is a woman's value dependent exclusively upon her role as a wife and mother?" The answer is simple and obvious—no!

Although rearing children to walk in righteousness is one of the most far-reaching and eternal impacts we can have on a spirit sent from our Heavenly Father, motherhood and marital status are not the only measures of a woman's worth, just as fatherhood and marital status are not the only measure of a man's worth.

Some women do not have the privilege of marrying or rearing children in this life. To the faithful, these blessings will come later. Of course, some women nurture children by adopting them, teaching and training them as sisters, aunts, teachers, advisers, and stepmothers, or influencing them through many volunteer opportunities wherein adult women bless young children's lives.

Motherhood is eternal with Godhood, and there is no such thing as eternal or endless life without the eternal and endless continuation of motherhood.
—Melvin J. Ballard

Men and women who do have the privilege of rearing children will, of course, be held accountable for that priceless, eternal stewardship. Although there is simply not a more significant contribution you can make to society, to the Church, or to the eternal destiny of our Father's children than what you will do as a mother or father, motherhood and fatherhood are not the only measure of goodness or of one's acceptance before the Lord. Every righteous man and woman has a significant role to play in the onward march of the kingdom of God.

I have a deep and abiding feeling about women and about the crucial difference they make in every important setting—particularly in the family and in the Church. I have spoken boldly about the role women must play in the council system of the Church. We cannot fulfill our mission as a Church without the inspired insight and real-life experiences of women.

I once wrote about an experience I had several years ago when assigned to attend a stake conference in Europe:

> When I arrived at the stake center I met the stake Relief Society president, who was busy preparing some refreshments for the stake presidency and me. I took occasion to visit with her privately to thank her for her faithful service. While we were talking, I asked her how she was feeling about her calling in the Church. "Elder Ballard," she said, her voice edged with exasperation, "will the brethren in leadership positions ever understand that the sisters want to make a contribution to the real issues facing the Church and its members?"
>
> As you might expect, I was a little surprised at her answer and the palpable frustration that clearly had prompted it. So I asked her to elaborate. "Sometimes I feel like the hired help at the council table," she said. "I'm there to serve, but not to contribute. When they talk about ways to accomplish the mission of the Church, my opinion is never sought. And when they refer to the decisions of stake leaders, they never acknowledge me as a leader who can make contribution to the spiritual growth and development of stake members. Sometimes they even talk about ways to meet the needs of the sisters in our stake without even inviting me to participate. I'm given assignments, and I do what I'm told. But I never feel that I am asked to *counsel.* And I was wondering: Is that the way it's supposed to work?"
>
> My first thought was: "How can this be? She is a member of the stake council and the leader of the Relief Society in her stake. How can she feel that she is not a part of things?" I assured her that it was not the Lord's program to ignore the magnificent spiritual capabilities of those who have been called through inspiration to preside over stake and ward

> Relief Society, Young Women, and Primary organizations. Indeed, God has inspired the creation of a council system that is intended to harness the insight and experience of all who have been called to serve in key leadership positions in the ward and stake. (*Counseling with Our Councils,* 1–2)

We need you faithful women to participate fully in our councils! We need women to participate fully in the work of salvation.

Because you can and do play an important role in bringing about much righteousness (see Doctrine and Covenants 58:27–28), I am concerned about what I see happening with some of our young people. Satan would have you dress, talk, and behave in unnatural and destructive ways in your relationships with those of the opposite sex. The adversary is having a heyday distorting attitudes about gender and roles and about families and individual worth. He is the author of mass confusion about the value, role, contribution, and unique nature of women and men. Today's popular culture, which is preached by every form of media from the silver screen to the Internet, celebrates the sexy, saucy, socially aggressive woman and man. These distortions are seeping into the thinking of some of our own young people.

> *While I recognize that this is the greatest age truth has ever known, there is always danger that in the desire for change many tried and worthy standards may be discarded; but the moral standards set up by this Church are standards which must remain and which cannot be changed or modified without disaster to us.*
> —MELVIN J. BALLARD

My deep desire is to clarify how we in the presiding councils of the Church feel about the sisters of this Church, how our Heavenly Father feels about His daughters, and what He expects of them. My dear sisters, we believe in you. We believe in and are counting on your goodness and your strength, your propensity for virtue and valor, your kindness and courage, your stability and resilience, and your significant contributions to hasten the work of the Lord as fellow laborers in the vineyard. We believe in your mission as women of God. We realize that you are the emotional (and sometimes spiritual) glue that holds families and often ward families together. We know you contribute to the financial well-being of families in significant ways, and, in some cases, carry the load to support the family entirely on your own shoulders.

Your contributions to the kingdom are immeasurable and diverse. We believe that the Church simply will not accomplish what it must without your faith and faithfulness, your innate tendency to put the wellbeing of others ahead of your own, your inspired leadership and mentoring of a new generation of young Church members, and your spiritual strength and tenacity to bless others, both men and women.

And we believe that God's plan is for you to become queens and to receive the highest blessings any woman can receive in time or eternity—whereas Satan's plan is to get you so preoccupied with the world's glitzy lies about women that you completely miss what you have come here to do and to become. Remember, he wants us to "be miserable like unto himself" (2 Nephi 2:27). Never lose your precious identity by doing anything that would jeopardize the promised eternal future your Heavenly Father has provided for you.

> *I know the testimony of thousands and have proven it in my own experience, that there is no life lived on this earth that is so happy, so full of joy and satisfaction, so abundant in health and life, so great in spirituality and true intelligence, as that enjoyed by the Latter-day Saints who live up to . . . gospel standards.*
>
> —Melvin J. Ballard

My earnest plea and prayer are that both men and women will understand that our sisters have always been vital and integral to the work of the Lord. Men must counsel with women, and men must respect and seek women's inspired insights. Women's voices must be heard in the Church councils and in our classrooms, and women must be seen doing the work of the Lord.

It's clear from the revelation given to Emma Smith in 1830 that the Lord needs, wants, and encourages women to become more than they may have felt possible (see Doctrine and Covenants 25, especially vv. 6–10). He desires all of His children, both men and women, to develop their talents to bless His other children.

Faithful women have labored valiantly in the cause of truth and righteousness from before the foundations of this world. In President Joseph F. Smith's vision of the redemption of the dead, he saw not only Father Adam and other prophets but also "our glorious Mother Eve, with many of her faithful daughters who had lived through the ages and worshiped the true and living God" (Doctrine and Covenants 138:39).

Think about the incomparable role of Eve, whose actions set in motion the great plan of our Father. Consider the example of other Old Testament women, such as the matriarchs Sarah (wife of Abraham), Rebekah (wife of Isaac), and Leah and Rachel (wives of Jacob), as well as other heroines mentioned in scripture, such as Ruth and Esther.

And what about Mary, the "precious and chosen vessel" (Alma 7:10) who bore the Christ child? There are other New Testament women, including Mary Magdalene, Joanna, Priscilla, and Junia, who made a difference in the lives of people they met (see Luke 8:2–3 and Romans 16). Surely no one would question the contributions made by those noble and faithful women.

These women served as examples of discipleship. In fact, Isaiah invited Israel to "Look" not only "unto Abraham, your father," but "unto Sarah, she that bare you" (2 Nephi 8:2; see also Isaiah 51:2).

Our dispensation is not without its heroines. Countless women from every continent and walk of life have made dramatic contributions to the cause of Christ. Consider Lucy Mack Smith, the mother of the martyred prophets Joseph and Hyrum and the grandmother of President Joseph F. Smith. Her resilience and righteousness under the most emotionally and spiritually taxing conditions surely influenced her prophet sons and set them firmly on the path toward fulfilling their foreordained destiny. Other Restoration heroines include Eliza R. Snow, Emmeline B. Wells, Martha Hughes Cannon, and many lesser-known women.

At this point you may be thinking, "But what about me and my contribution? I'm not Eve or Mary or Lucy Mack Smith or even a nineteenth-century Mormon woman pioneer. I'm just regular, plain old me. Is there something about my contribution that is significant to the Lord? Does He really need me?" Remember, the righteous who are not highly visible are valued too, and, in the words of a Book of Mormon prophet, they are "no less serviceable unto the people" (Alma 48:19).

President Spencer W. Kimball counseled us as follows: "Both a righteous man and a righteous woman are a blessing to all those whom their lives touch. . . . [In] the world before we came here, faithful women were given certain assignments while faithful men were foreordained to certain priesthood tasks. While we do not now remember the particulars . . . we are accountable for those things which long ago were expected of us" (*My Beloved Sisters,* 37).

> *There is no member in the Church who has not made great and important promises to the Lord [to] keep His commandments and walk in His paths. . . . A promise that we make to the Lord should be just as faithfully fulfilled as any promise we make to our fellow men.*
> —HYRUM MACK SMITH

Every woman in this Church who has made covenants with the Lord has a divine mandate to help save souls, lead the women of the world, strengthen the homes of Zion, make a difference in her neighborhood, community, and nation, and build the kingdom of God. Eliza R. Snow, the second general president of the Relief Society, said that "every sister in this church should be a preacher of righteousness . . . because we have greater and higher privileges than any other females upon the face of the earth" ("Great Indignation Meeting," 2).

Every sister who stands for truth and righteousness diminishes the influence of evil. Every sister who strengthens and protects her family and the Church is doing the work of God. Every sister who lives as a woman of God becomes a beacon for others to follow and plants seeds of righteous influence that will be harvested for decades to come. Every sister who "invite[s] others to come unto Christ by helping them receive the restored gospel through faith in Jesus Christ and His Atonement, repentance, baptism, receiving the gift of the Holy Ghost, and enduring to the end" is helping hasten the work of the Lord (*Preach My Gospel*, 1). Every sister who makes and keeps sacred covenants becomes an instrument in the hands of God.

> *We should not enter thoughtlessly and hastily into sacred promises either with God or man, but it should be done after due deliberation. Then, when it is done, we should have a determination that so far as we are concerned that promise shall be sacredly and faithfully kept.*
> —Hyrum Mack Smith

I have been drawn to an interchange between God the Father and His Only Begotten Son, who is the ultimate example of living up to one's premortal promises. When God asked who would come to earth to prepare a way for all mankind to be saved and strengthened and blessed, it was Jesus Christ who said, simply, "Here am I, send me" (Abraham 3:27).

Just as the Savior stepped forward to fulfill His divine responsibilities, we have the invitation and responsibility to do likewise. If you are wondering if you make a difference to the Lord, imagine the impact when you make commitments such as the following:

"Father, if you need a woman to visit the widow and fatherless, here am I, send me."

"If you need a woman to rear children in righteousness, here am I, send me."

"Father, if you need a faithful woman who can stand as a witness of Jesus Christ and His restored gospel, here am I, send me."

"If you need a woman who will shun vulgarity and dress modestly and speak with dignity and show the world how joyous it is to keep the commandments, here am I, send me."

"Father, if you need a woman who can resist the alluring temptations of the world by keeping her eyes fixed on eternity, here am I, send me."

"If you need a woman of faithful steadiness, here am I, send me."

"If you need a woman to participate fully in family, ward, and stake councils, here am I, send me."

May the Lord bless the people and give them understanding and great faith. May they be full of the Holy Ghost, that they may see and know and understand the things of God, and walk uprightly and honestly in the straight and narrow way, all the days of their lives, and let their example be seen.

—HYRUM MACK SMITH

Finally, "Lord, if you need a woman who will succor the weak, lift up the hands which hang down, and strengthen the feeble knees, here am I, send me."

Between now and the day the Lord comes again, He needs women in every family, in every ward, in every community, in every nation who will step forward in righteousness and say by their words and their actions, "Here am I, send me."

My question is, will you be one of those women? And will you men answer the same call? I feel quite sure that you want to. But how will you do it? In a world filled with deceptive messages about women and the family, knowing the significance of both to the

Lord, *how* will you perpetually respond to the Lord, "Here am I, send me"?

> *If one of us were to take a trip by automobile across the continent, we would be very willing to follow the suggestions of a perfect stranger who has been over the road, and if he advised us to take the left-hand road at a certain point, although it would seem the rougher road, we would undoubtedly follow him, because he has been over the road. Why are we not as wise about all things? Life is a journey over which we have never been before, and we shall never go again. Yet someone has been over the road.*
> —Melvin J. Ballard

The Prophet Joseph Smith invited the sisters to "live up to [their] privilege" (as quoted in *Daughters in My Kingdom*, 171).

If you really want to live up to your privilege, I have two suggestions: First, learn to hear the voice of the Spirit, or the voice of the Lord as communicated by the power of the Holy Ghost. Second, listen to and follow those whom we sustain as prophets, seers, and revelators.

I cannot stress enough the importance of listening to and following the prophet and the apostles. In today's world, where twenty-four hours a day the media's talking heads spew forth conflicting opinions, where men and women jockey for everything from your money to your vote, there is one clear, unpolluted, unbiased voice that you can always count on. And that is the voice of the Lord as revealed to the world through His living prophet and apostles (see Doctrine and Covenants 1:38). The Lord's only motive, hence His servants' only motive, is "the everlasting welfare of your souls" (2 Nephi 2:30).

Think of it! Think about the value of having a source of information that you can always count on, that will always have your eternal interests at heart, and that will always provide inspired truth. That's a phenomenal gift and guide.

I make you a promise. It is a simple one, but it is true. If you will listen to the Lord as He reveals His will, counsel, and direction through His living prophet and apostles, and if you will heed our counsel, you will not go astray.

I have come to learn that if you want to avoid the snares of Satan, and if you need direction when the choices in front of you are puzzling and perplexing, learn to hear the voice of the Lord as communicated through the Holy Ghost. And then, of course, do what the Spirit tells you to do.

Nephi taught clearly that the Holy Ghost is "the gift of God unto all those who diligently seek him" and that "he that diligently seeketh shall find" (1 Nephi 10:17, 19). The stunning reality is that you control how close you are to the Lord. You determine just how clear and readily available promptings from the Holy Ghost will be. You determine this by your actions, by your attitude, by the choices you make, by the things you watch and wear and listen to and read, and by how consistently and sincerely you invite the Spirit into your life.

Contemplate for a moment the extent and the impact of this blessing! You have been given a gift that when exercised and respected will give you the answers to all the confusing, thorny questions and problems you will face in your life.

When I was a young bishop, one of the sisters in my ward was an elderly widow who was living with her daughter's family. She was in frail health. I called on her often. We had a wonderful, easy relationship and could joke and laugh together. One evening in the wintertime, I left the bishop's office about ten o'clock at night to go home. I had a strong impression to go visit this sister. It was late, I was tired, and it was snowing. I rationalized that it would be best not to disturb her at such a late hour and decided to get a good night's sleep and visit her first thing the next morning. I went to bed but did not rest well.

Early the next morning, I went to see this dear sister. When her daughter came to the door, it was obvious that she had been crying. She greeted me with the words, "Oh, Bishop, thank you for coming. Mother passed away two hours ago."

This faithful sister deserved to have her bishop hold her hand and give her a blessing of peace and comfort as her mortal life came to an end. I missed the opportunity because I didn't act. I determined that this painful lesson would never have to be repeated. Since that time, I have tried to listen to and act on promptings as they have been received.

This we know, that God lives and that those who place their trust in Him are under His protecting care. It is not necessary that we should know the details of the future. We are all passengers on the stormy ocean of life, speeding towards the shore of eternity. . . . We only know that our Captain is capable of meeting all emergencies, and that, if we conform to the rules of the ship, all will be well with us, and we shall reach the harbor in safety.
—HYRUM MACK SMITH

As life progresses, how will you respond to challenges that will inevitably come? Will you know where to turn for peace and consolation if you are called upon to bury a child—as two of our own children have done—or if a child threatens to stray from the gospel path? How will you know what to do when you face financial reverses? Where will you turn for insight and inspiration when you are called upon to lead in your ward or stake? These questions are important for both women and men to consider.

There are several principles that greatly enhance our ability to understand the promptings of the Holy Ghost and thereby hear the voice of God.

The first is fasting and prayer. When the sons of Mosiah were united with Alma the Younger, they rejoiced in their reunion and acknowledged that because they had "given themselves to much prayer, and fasting" they had been gifted with the spirit of prophecy and revelation. "And when they taught, they taught with power and authority of God" (Alma 17:3).

The second is immersing yourself in the scriptures. The word of God "will tell you all things what ye should do" (2 Nephi 32:3). The scriptures are a conduit for personal revelation. You have been taught to read and study the scriptures. I urge you to intensify your study of them by reading, understanding, and applying the scriptures. I promise that your ability to hear the voice of the Lord as communicated through the Holy Ghost will increase and improve.

The third is spending time in the house of the Lord. When we attend the temple, we come out "armed with power" (Doctrine and Covenants 109:22) and with the promise that as we "grow up" in our knowledge of the Lord, we will "receive a fulness of the Holy Ghost" (Doctrine and Covenants 109:15). The temple is a place of personal revelation. If you can obtain a limited use recommend, attend the temple to perform baptisms for the dead. If you are endowed, visit the temple regularly. If you are not ready, prepare yourself to enter, and visit the temple grounds often.

The temple grounds are sacred and have been dedicated to the Lord by His prophets. If you will turn off your cell phones and put away your social media devices, you can find a measure of peace and quiet that will allow you to think about the things of eternity. On the temple grounds you will feel His presence, and this will give you a desire to enter the house of the Lord as soon as you are able to do so. Inside the doors of the temple are the covenants and promises that will give you the strength, power, and encouragement to remain faithful to the end. In the temple you will be "endowed with power from on high"

No one understood the secret power obtained through fasting and prayer better than the Master Himself, who, prior to the commencement of His ministry, went into the wilderness, where He fasted forty days. . . . Surely if He, who was perfect, found added blessings through fasting and prayer, who is there among us who can excuse himself from the observance of this commandment?

—Melvin J. Ballard

(Doctrine and Covenants 38:32)—a power that will fortify you against the vicissitudes of life.

Fourth is obedience and repentance. You simply cannot do certain things if you want to have the Holy Ghost with you as a constant companion. It is not possible to listen to vulgar lyrics, watch movies filled with sexual innuendo, tamper with pornography, take the name of the Lord in vain, wear revealing clothing, compromise in any way the law of chastity, or disregard the values of true manhood and womanhood and expect the Holy Ghost to remain with you always.

> *We get our reward here and now. Our joy, our achievements, have brought us heaven right now, and it is preparing us for an eternal heaven that is yet to come.*
> —Melvin J. Ballard

Whenever anyone participates in those kinds of activities, it should not be a surprise if feelings of loneliness, discouragement, and unworthiness follow. Do not make the choice to go it alone rather than have the Spirit of the Lord to guide, protect, prompt, warn, and fill you with peace. Repent if you need to so you can enjoy the companionship of the Spirit more fully in your life.

Women and men who hear the voice of the Lord and who respond to those promptings become invaluable instruments in His hands. I will never forget an experience I had following a stake conference. I was asked to participate in a blessing for a young woman who was suffering with cancer. The family members were converts to the Church, and they had found peace through the promptings of the Spirit. Prior to our giving the blessing, this dear sister said to me: "Elder Ballard, I am not afraid to die, but I would like to live here with my family. I am prepared to accept the will of my Father in Heaven. Please bless me to find peace and to know that He will be with me." What faith, insight, and courage the Spirit had blessed her with! A few months later, the family advised me that Heavenly Father had called her home. She died in peace, and the family lived in peace because they were familiar with the Spirit. One of the sweetest messages the Spirit will relay is how the Lord feels about you. And that reassurance will strengthen you in a way that almost nothing else can.

Now finally, I turn again to you dear sisters, you who have such a profound, innate spiritual ability to hear the voice of the Good Shepherd. I pray that you will never wonder again if you have worth in the sight of the Lord and to those He has called to preside in the Church for a season. We love you. We cherish you. We respect you. We need you. We want you to participate fully in the work of salvation.

> *Our trust is in the Lord. Upon Him we depend, and we look in faith unto Him to give us strength and wisdom and the inspiration of the Holy Spirit to accomplish with success, and to His name's honor and glory, the work He has called us to do.*
>
> —Hyrum Mack Smith

Never doubt that your influence is absolutely vital to preserving the family and to assisting with the growth and spiritual vitality of the kingdom of God on earth. The Church will not reach its foreordained destiny without you. We men rarely nurture like you nurture. Most of us don't have the sensitivity, spiritual and otherwise, that by your eternal nature you inherently have. Your influence on families and with children, with youth, and with men and other women is singular. Because of your unusual gifts and talents, you are vital to taking the gospel to all the world, to demonstrating that there is joy in living the way the Lord has counseled us to live.

More than ever before we need women of faith, virtue, vision, and charity, as the Relief Society declaration proclaims. We need women who can hear and will respond to the voice of the Lord, women who at all costs will defend and protect the family and the Church. We need women who rejoice in their womanhood and have a spiritual confirmation of their identity, their value, and their eternal destiny. Above all, we need women who will stand up for truth and righteousness, decry evil at every turn, and simply say, "Lord, here am I, send me."

CHAPTER 7

Building Kinder, Gentler Homes

After death, that which existed before and independent of the body will continue, until through the resurrection of the earthly body the union of spirit and matter will take place, providing the power and ability to touch and know all realms. . . . It is not hard to think of man as an eternal being, who through the grace of Jesus Christ, our Lord, shall come forth from the grave into the newness of life and shall dwell with Him in the heavens.

—Melvin J. Ballard

Some years ago, our little four-and-a-half-month-old granddaughter was called to end her mission in mortality. As you might imagine, this experience evoked some very tender feelings in my grandfather heart. I did a great deal of reading. I read sermons by those who had been called upon to try to bring comfort into the lives of people who have lost a dear one—and especially a tiny one.

As we visited our precious granddaughter in the hospital before her passing, I held her hand and talked to her as a grandfather would. I had the peaceful assurance come to me that this little girl would be ours, even though she would not stay on earth much longer. Into my mind came the words, as though spoken by her to me, "Don't worry, Grandpa, I'll be all right." Peace came into my heart. The Master's touch fell upon all of us.

As I went through that process, I was overwhelmed with the blessing we have as members of the Church of Jesus Christ. I can't contemplate what it must be like to face the loss of a loved one without having the gospel, without knowing the eternal nature of the spirit, without understanding the total purpose for life. I can't imagine what families must think, the questions that must go through their minds without answers, when they are without the gospel of Jesus Christ.

[My father] exemplified in a most wonderful degree the principles of justice and impartiality among the members of his household . . . so that it could not be discovered that any one of them was held more dearly and more closely in his affections than any other. . . . He loved them all with a love akin to the love of God for His children.
—Hyrum Mack Smith

I came to a new resolve in my own heart as I had unfolded to me, in perhaps clearer terms than at any other time in my life, the divine nature of the human soul. I acquired a new appreciation for the precious importance of every living son and daughter of God, the intense interest that Heavenly Father has in each of our lives, the understanding that He loves us, that we belong to Him, and that we have an eternal Mother as well. We are eternal in nature; they begat us spiritually. Nothing happens in our lives except as our Father in Heaven would have it happen, inasmuch as we strive to keep His commandments.

I have always been impressed with a statement made by President George H. W. Bush in his inaugural address. He said, "Our purpose today is to make kinder the face of the nation and gentler the face of the world." I believe that wonderful vision can be realized only if the homes of the world become kinder and gentler, worthy abodes for the precious sons and daughters of our Heavenly Father. Fathers and mothers and children must foster the spirit of gentleness and kindness within the walls of their own homes. It is troubling to see the difficulty some families have in living together in love and thus being able to get out of life the fulness that the gospel of Jesus Christ offers them.

It is not unusual for a Church leader to have a troubled youth want to talk to him or her. Sometimes a young man or young woman will have had serious difficulties in his or her life that require clearance by a General Authority so the young man or woman can serve a mission. When I interview young people who have committed transgression of a moral nature, I always inquire about the kind of direction they received from their parents. It is disheartening to have a youth respond, "Well, we never talked about that." It is even worse when they respond, "I can't talk to my father or mother about these kinds of personal concerns or worries." Homes based on the foundation of the teachings of Jesus should never have a circumstance in which children feel uncomfortable talking to their parents about life's issues and challenges.

> *Every doctrine of the gospel and every precept imparted in this Church tends to exalt, and uplift, and ennoble men and women and make them better, purer, and more righteous men and women, more devoted, and full of integrity, loyalty, and faithfulness both to God and to man. . . . This is the kind of fathers and mothers the gospel teaches men and women to be.*
>
> —HYRUM MACK SMITH

Is there a need for greater kindness in your home? I hope we do not have many fathers or mothers in the Church who raise their voices within the walls of their own homes. But just in case there might be a father or mother who has that difficulty, may I call upon you to take hold of that matter in your life and stay under control? Have the courage today to make a resolve in your heart to change. Don't yell at your children. Don't say angry or mean things to your spouse. Foster the kinder and gentler attitude.

The Lord gave us direction on how we interact with each other—at home, school, work, church, and in our communities:

> Behold, there are many called, but few are chosen. And why are they not chosen?
>
> Because their hearts are set so much upon the things of this world, and aspire to the honors of men, that they do not learn this one lesson—
>
> That the rights of the priesthood are inseparably connected with the powers of heaven, and that the powers of heaven cannot be controlled nor handled only upon the principles of righteousness.
>
> That they may be conferred upon us, it is true; but when we undertake to cover our sins, or to gratify our pride, our vain ambition, or to exercise control or dominion or compulsion upon the souls of the children of men, in any degree of unrighteousness, behold, the heavens withdraw themselves; the Spirit of the Lord is grieved; and when it is withdrawn, Amen to the priesthood or the authority of that man. (Doctrine and Covenants 121:34–37)

As you mold [your children], as you fashion them, as you develop them, so shall they be; and your name shall be written upon the tablets of their memory.
—Melvin J. Ballard

I believe that when a father loses his temper and becomes angry, his power of the priesthood ceases to function to the benefit and blessing of his family. The same is true of a mother who loses her temper; she weakens the moral authority of her role as a parent and is less able to bless her family when needed.

When fathers and mothers can teach by the power of the Spirit in a gentler and kinder way, I believe they will see increased unity within the family and a much better response to their teachings.

May I suggest to you fathers and mothers a simple thing you might want to consider, especially if you are not already doing it. This is something you might want to do to help you be a better dad or mom. Are you really close to your children? Are you interviewing them—in the sense that you are sitting down and having a good visit on a regular basis? This can be particularly important for moms or dads who are away from home much of the time because of work, Church assignments, or extended family needs.

[My father] always has been very conscientious in the care and protection that he bestowed upon . . . his children, and religiously endeavored to instruct them in the ways of truth and righteousness. He has taught his children from their infancy to be truthful and honest, to be virtuous and chaste, to be kind and just and merciful, to be temperate and sober and obedient.
—HYRUM MACK SMITH

Are you praying individually with your children over problems in their lives that perhaps only Heavenly Father can solve? Some of the most impressive experiences that occurred with our seven children were those magic moments when I found myself with just one of my daughters or sons as we knelt quietly in the study or in my office at home and as I held that child's hand and supplicated a special blessing on his or her behalf. As they grew older and began bearing and bringing forth their own children, it was a joy to have them say to me, "Do you have any idea how important those few minutes were, Dad, that we spent on our knees, just the two of us, talking to our Father in Heaven?"

When one of my daughters was in high school, she came to me one afternoon around three o'clock and said, "Daddy, I have been studying for about thirty-five hours for a test in chemistry tomorrow, and I just simply do not understand. I have done everything I know how and I am confused. It is vague in my mind, and I know that when I sit down to take that test tomorrow, I am going to fail it. Can you help me?"

I said, "Well, sweetheart, let me tell you about your dad and chemistry. When I studied at East High School, my companion and I were in the laboratory, and we thought we were following instructions from the teacher. He was having us mix some ingredients, and we thought we were doing the right thing. Then, at the appropriate time, he asked us to light the test tube so the ingredients we put into it would burn. And everybody's burned except ours. Ours exploded! The bottom end of the test tube was in one of those racks, and it shot across the laboratory into the wall. I can still see Mr. Howells running down to us with his hands in the air, awfully upset, yelling, 'Boys, boys, what have you done?'"

> *One of the most important responsibilities resting upon parents is that they shall see to it that no child goes out from their home that has not had planted in its heart in its tender years a love of prayer, and ability to pray, and that the practice and the spirit of prayer is inculcated in its heart in that home training.*
> —Melvin J. Ballard

And then I looked at my little seventeen-year-old and said, "Sweetheart, to this day, I don't know what we put into our test tube that was any different from all the rest of the kids in that class, and you've come to me to ask me to help you with chemistry. We are in real trouble. The only thing I know I can do in the time frame you have left is for us to go into the office and kneel down and ask the Lord to bless you. Would you like that?"

"Would you do that, Daddy?"

I said, "It would be an honor."

We then went into the office and knelt down. What a thrill to hold the hand of my teenage daughter and supplicate a special blessing from Heavenly Father. As her earthly father and steward, I had been entrusted by our Eternal Father to give her the assistance and the guidance that I could.

So we called upon Heavenly Father. We acknowledged Him as the great chemist. We acknowledged that He knew the beginning from the end. We did not ask for a miracle. We simply asked that Heavenly Father enlighten my daughter's mind and that somehow, by the power of the Holy Ghost, He would bring back to her remembrance what she had studied thirty-five hours for, that she might be successful in the test that she was to take the next day. We got up, and as we got on our feet, she threw her arms around my neck and gave me a kiss. As we stood there, tears were in our eyes while we concluded that very special father-daughter experience.

She went off to school the next day with a degree of confidence. Two or three days later she called me at home and said, "Dad"—I could tell by the inflection in her voice that she had good news—"guess what?"

"What, Honey?"

"I passed the test, and furthermore, Dad, I got the third highest score in the whole class. Dad, I don't know any more about chemistry now than I did before I took the test, but I passed!"

I was impressed at that moment, a sacred, special, father's moment, to teach a principle. "Sweetheart, you might not know any more about chemistry, but you know a lot more about your Heavenly Father. He has blessed you as we supplicated Him to do."

I pray, then, my dear brethren and sisters who are parents, that you might have the wisdom to not feel obligated to know the answers to all things in the lives of your children. There are many questions that will come to you from your children that perhaps you can't answer, but you can pray for guidance, you can pray for help, and you can pray for direction, which is a blessing Heavenly Father will grant to all His children who humbly go before Him.

> *Why did the Master pray? Though He were the Son of God, no man of whom we have any record ever was a greater praying man than the Redeemer himself. Wherever He had the opportunity, He was constantly slipping away by Himself and opening His soul to His Father in prayer. If He, the Matchless One, needed this help, this strength, and these blessings, what of us?*
>
> —Melvin J. Ballard

We know from section 121 of the Doctrine and Covenants

that the Prophet Joseph Smith received from the Lord a very interesting principle. I think, brethren, we have to be very careful about this because sometimes we can have the misconception that because we hold the priesthood, that entitles us to be a ruler or a king within the dominion of our own homes. Yes, we have the priesthood and have the responsibility to preside. But the Lord has told us very clearly how that responsibility should be used:

> We have learned by sad experience [remember this is the Lord speaking to the Prophet Joseph] that it is the nature and disposition of almost all men, as soon as they get a little authority, as they suppose, they will immediately begin to exercise unrighteous dominion.
>
> Hence many are called, but few are chosen. (Doctrine and Covenants 121:39–40)

As the physical instruments of men, devised to catch the messages that come from a distance, must be in tune with the sending instrument, so we must be in tune with God, with His Spirit, with His truth. If we catch the message, we must be in tune, and prayer tends to bring us in tune.
—Melvin J. Ballard

Let us use our priesthood authority wisely, brethren.

Now I'll add the women to the discussion of the next verses because, to me, if we could get these principles operating within the walls of our own homes, we would become kinder and gentler in our dealings with one another. In this process, we will become more spiritually in tune.

The Lord said:

> No power or influence can or ought to be maintained by virtue of the priesthood, only by persuasion, by long-suffering, by gentleness and meekness, and by love unfeigned [I think those principles apply to both men and women];

By kindness, and pure knowledge, which shall greatly enlarge the soul without hypocrisy, and without guile—

Reproving betimes with sharpness, when moved upon by the Holy Ghost; and then showing forth afterwards an increase of love toward him whom thou hast reproved, lest he esteem thee to be his enemy;

That he may know that thy faithfulness is stronger than the cords of death.

Let thy bowels also be full of charity towards all men, and to the household of faith, and let virtue garnish thy thoughts unceasingly; then shall thy confidence wax strong in the presence of God; and the doctrine of the priesthood shall distil upon thy soul as the dews from heaven.

The Holy Ghost shall be thy constant companion, and thy scepter an unchanging scepter of righteousness and truth; and thy dominion shall be an everlasting dominion, and without compulsory means it shall flow unto thee forever and ever. (Doctrine and Covenants 121:41–46)

The covenants we take in the house of God make an impression upon our hearts, as great as life itself, and more enduring than mortal life. . . . Jealousy, human weaknesses, frailties, mistakes must be tolerated and borne with in love and patience. We are all subject more or less to these human frailties, and we expect that those given to each other in the holy bonds of matrimony will be tolerant, kind and long suffering.
—Hyrum Mack Smith

God bless all of us, brethren and sisters, in our sacred roles as fathers and mothers, that we will be very careful how we conduct ourselves within the walls of our own homes.

Sisters, it is possible that we have a mother here and there who has a tendency to lose her temper and raise her voice while raising her children. One mother, when I mentioned this, said, "Brother Ballard, if you had my children, you would understand why I lose my temper." Stay calm, sisters. You can do it! I received a beautiful letter from a mother who confessed that she had this problem. She said she had an awful time keeping her temper under control. She was frustrated most of the time in her role of mothering. She made a promise to her Heavenly Father that somehow she was going to overcome this in her life. In her letter, she said she wasn't perfect yet, but she was a lot better. She expressed her gratitude for the serenity, kindness, and gentleness that was developing in their home.

> *If we value the innocence, virtue, and purity of our youth, then we should see to it that their innocence, virtue, and purity are guarded, that our children are kept away from contaminating influences, and that such influences are kept away from them, just as far as lies in our power.*
> —HYRUM MACK SMITH

Sisters, sometimes I think you feel like you have to be "super mom." I ask you to not feel that way. Just be calm and gentle and approachable. And be there for the appropriate needs of your husband and your children—just as your husband and children need to be there to meet your appropriate needs.

If you need to adjust your goals a little for a season, I say to you, adjust them. But in the process, be sure you adjust the things that matter least and intensify the things that matter most. Build a kinder and gentler home.

We must be on guard about what we are exposed to on television and the Internet. Electronic "entertainment" can disturb, upset, and confuse the gentleness in our homes. Parents, know what your children are watching. Media can be an insidious tool of the evil one if not controlled. Media can destroy the love and peace we all want in our homes.

Now, a word to children. The Lord taught:

> Children, obey your parents in the Lord: for this is right.
> *Honour thy father and mother;* (which is the first commandment with promise;)

> That it may be well with thee, and that thou mayest live long on the earth.
>
> And, ye fathers, provoke not your children to wrath: but bring them up in the nurture and admonition of the Lord. (Ephesians 6:1–4; emphasis added)

You have every right as a child to be heard. But there is a right way to have a discussion with your father or mother. If your parents have imposed some kind of a rule that you don't agree with, don't fight, or yell, or go off and pout, or slam the door to your bedroom and think that that is going to correct the problem. Rather, in a mature way, say, "Mom and Dad, I have a problem I am struggling with. We have a rule that I don't understand, or I don't agree with, and I would like to have a discussion and have you help me understand better why the rule stands as it does." You do not have the right to raise your voice and be ugly in word or action to your father or mother. Neither do they have the right to raise their voices and be ugly in word or action to you.

> *How closely do we, sons and daughters of faithful fathers and mothers, observe this commandment? Do we return unto them the homage that is their due, the honor they are entitled to? Do we heed their counsel, and take their advice?*
>
> —Hyrum Mack Smith

Let me tell you two stories that might help you. Sometimes children will say, "Well, Brother Ballard, that is all well and good, but my father just won't give me that kind of attention." When our oldest daughter was about six or seven years old (a sweet girl who is now the mother of six of our grandchildren), she came to me as I was reading the newspaper. She asked me a question, and I was not paying attention as I should. She climbed up on my lap, grabbed the newspaper with both of her tiny hands and pulled it down, took hold of my face, and whipped it around so we were eye to eye. I can still see those big brown eyes as she said, "Daddy, you're not listening to me."

I said, "Sweetheart, let me listen."

When our oldest son was about two and a half, I came home from work one night and listened as Barbara informed me that there was a problem with him. I don't remember what it was that happened, but I had had a busy day. So I took him into the bedroom and sat him up on his bed and looked at him and started to give him some guidance and direction. I can see it as clearly as though it were yesterday. When I got through, his little chin started to quiver, and he said, "Daddy, I didn't do it."

Mind you, at this point in my life I had never been a father before, but I had the presence of mind to sweep him up in my arms and ask him to forgive me. Parents, perhaps one of the most vital and important principles that you and I need to understand is the principle of listening—being willing to listen with an open, kind, and gentle spirit.

Now, finally, a word to grandfathers and grandmothers. I've tried to decide what a grandpa is, now that I am one, with forty-three grandchildren and many, many great-grandchildren. What is important for us to do in our role as grandparents? I remember a great man in our ward who said in a testimony meeting, after he had just had all of his grandchildren at his home, "You never know what kind of a parent you have been until you see how your grandchildren turn out." That is quite profound.

I think grandparents ought to be memory makers. I think you

> *Let fathers and mothers throughout Israel set an example before their families; let them keep the commandments of the Lord, . . . so that the children, all the days of their lives, shall look upon father and mother with love and respect, and say in their hearts: We have the noblest father and the grandest mother that ever lived in the world.*
>
> —Hyrum Mack Smith

need to make memories that will live forever in the lives of your grandchildren. Do those little things you can in their lives that will endear you to them forever.

My Grandfather Ballard stood at the pulpit for twenty years as a member of the Quorum of the Twelve Apostles. He died when I was just ten years of age. I was not old enough or wise enough to realize who he was. He was just Grandpa, but a grandpa who loved me. On my eighth birthday, he took me to the Rialto Theatre to see a Walt Disney movie. We went into the theatre and sat down, the lights went off, and Grandfather fell fast asleep. He slept rather noisily, which bothered me. I couldn't understand how anybody could sleep through a Walt Disney movie. I watched the show through, and it started the second time. I had to shake him to wake him up. He got up and, as I recall, we got an ice cream cone and then went home. That is a memory I would certainly hate to have missed. It is a simple little thing, but it has lived so preciously with me all these years.

I recall coming home from an assignment and listening to my children as they lobbied that we go see *Star Wars* at the Center Theatre in Salt Lake City. I thought that would be fine and was assured it was a good movie. We went to the movie, the lights went off, and I fell fast asleep. My children still wonder how it is possible that Dad could ever sleep through *Star Wars.* Now I can tell you that it is an occupational hazard of a General Authority—whenever the lights go off, he will fall fast asleep. I didn't understand that when

> *My responsibilities are greater than those of the artist who paints on canvas or chisels with the mallet; and more enduring is my work. For the time will come, no matter how skillful are the creations of men, when the canvas will fade and the marble will disintegrate and go into the dust of the earth. But your models, that boy and girl, . . . are imperishable souls that never shall die, and your work . . . shall leave its impress upon them eternally.*
> —MELVIN J. BALLARD

I was eight. But I understand it now because a grandfather made a precious memory.

God bless you, my beloved brothers and sisters, to draw your families close to you. Make precious memories, memories of gentleness, memories of kindness, memories of love that live with you now and that will go with you into eternity.

I testify to you that Jesus Christ is the Son of God and that He is gentle, kind, and full of love. We perhaps will never fully comprehend in mortality His love for you and me. But I testify to you as one of His witnesses that He loves all women and men everywhere and expects Latter-day Saint families to be families of strength, love, and peace.

God bless you. May the peace of the Lord Jesus Christ be in your hearts. If you are at peace within yourself, peace will be in your home, and in your neighborhood, and peace and gentleness and kindness will be in every nation throughout the world.

CHAPTER 8

The Law of Sacrifice

One year my family and I visited Palmyra, Kirtland, and Nauvoo. We reviewed the early history of the Church on that trip and were reminded of the overwhelming sacrifices the founders of the Church made to establish the kingdom of God on earth in this last dispensation. It was particularly poignant for my family, as my mother's great-grandfather, Hyrum Smith, and his brother Joseph sacrificed all for the cause of Christ. In Nauvoo, we reflected on the scene where Joseph and Hyrum left their families to go to Carthage Jail. Hyrum reached down from his horse and gathered into his arms his little five-year-old son, Joseph F. Smith, my great-grandfather, and held him and kissed him and placed him gently back upon the ground. He then rode off with his brother to where they would lay down their lives for the cause of Christ.

> *My own dear little mother came from Scotland, trudged all the way across the plains, a girl thirteen years of age . . . with a firm resolve to serve God and keep His commandments. They were not afraid to pay the price.*
>
> —Melvin J. Ballard

Many others sacrificed much during these early years of the Church. Among my ancestry, Hyrum's wife, Mary Fielding Smith, crossed the plains as a widowed mother of two, enduring much. On my father's side, Henry Ballard, who arrived in Winter Quarters with only the clothes on his back, drove a flock of sheep across the plains to pay his way, suffering and enduring much in his three-and-a-half-month journey.

Reflecting upon our Church history focused my mind on the eternal nature of the law of sacrifice, which is a vital part of the gospel of Jesus Christ that was practiced in Old Testament, New Testament, and Book of Mormon times. The New Testament is especially interesting because it describes a span of time during which the law of sacrifice was practiced in two different ways. In the first half of the New Testament, it was practiced as outlined in the law of Moses. Then, through the Atonement of Christ, the law of Moses was fulfilled, and the practice of the law of sacrifice changed. It is helpful to understand how the law of sacrifice was practiced before and after the Atonement.

Usually, the first thing people think of when they hear "law of Moses" is animal sacrifice. The somewhat gruesome nature of blood sacrifice has led some people to ask, "How could such an activity have anything to do with the gospel of love?"

There are two major, eternal purposes for the law of sacrifice that we need to understand. These purposes applied to Adam and Eve, Abraham and Sarah, Moses and Zipporah, and the righteous men and women mentioned in the New Testament, and they apply to us today as we accept and live the law of sacrifice. The two major purposes are to test and prove us and to assist us in coming unto Christ.

We must keep the commandments, all of them, every one of them, every day of our lives, and then we will prove ourselves wise and of understanding hearts.
—Hyrum Mack Smith

President Lorenzo Snow describes the first purpose of the law of sacrifice: "The trials and temptations have been very great to many of our people, and more or less, perhaps, to all of us. The Lord seems to require some proof on our part, something to show that He can depend upon us when He wants us to accomplish certain things in His interest" (in Conference Report, October 1900, 2).

Throughout history, we learn of many righteous people who suffered trials and tribulations as a result of trying to serve the Lord Jesus Christ: Adam and Eve, Abel, Noah, Abraham, Job, Lehi and Sariah, Nephi, Abish, Abinadi, Mary Magdalene, Stephen, Peter, Paul, Lydia, Mormon, Moroni, Martin and Katharina Luther, John Wesley, Roger and Mary Williams, Joseph and Hyrum Smith, Bathsheba Smith and Vilate Kimball, and a host of others. One writer said it this way: "We see that every age has been a time of stress, war, conflict, and struggle. . . . Men have been continually tempted and pressed to make decisions about their loyalty to their religious beliefs; they have been repeatedly forced to examine their relationship to their Father in heaven—and, in fact, they have been tested again and again and again" (Victor B. Cline, "Handcart Pioneers," 90).

> *I am sure that it was not the thought of our Heavenly Father that He would issue certain mandates to us just to see us in action, to discover whether or not we should be competent. I am sure that every requirement that He has made was essential to prepare us to come into His presence.*
> —Melvin J. Ballard

The Lord Himself spoke of proving and trying us: "I have decreed in my heart, saith the Lord, that *I will prove you in all things, whether you will abide in my covenant,* even unto death, that you may be found worthy. For if ye will not abide in my covenant ye are not worthy of me" (Doctrine and Covenants 98:14–15; emphasis added).

In describing his life of trials, the Prophet Joseph said: "I am like a huge, rough stone rolling down from a high mountain; and the only polishing I get is when some corner gets rubbed off by coming in contact with something else, striking with accelerated force, . . . knocking off a corner here and a corner there. Thus I will become a smooth and polished shaft in the quiver of the Almighty" (*Teachings of the Prophet Joseph Smith,* 304).

The law of sacrifice also provides an opportunity for us to prove to the Lord that we love Him more than any other thing. As a result, the course sometimes becomes difficult—but understandably so because this is the process of perfection that prepares us for the celestial kingdom to "dwell in the presence of God and his Christ forever and ever" (Doctrine and Covenants 76:62). How important it is for full-time missionaries to understand this principle before serving the Lord on their missions. Obedience to mission guidelines would automatically be part of every missionary's life if the law of sacrifice were correctly understood.

> *I recall being impressed when the call came to leave the business that I had built up, and that was so profitable, to go out to the Northwest [as mission president]. I suffered financial loss, and some of my associates thought it was foolish. I remarked that had the sacrifice been ten times as great, it would be no sacrifice for me to leave it, because I owed the Lord more than I could ever pay him if I gave him my whole life.*
> —Melvin J. Ballard

Now let us turn to the second purpose of the law of sacrifice, that of coming unto Christ. President Ezra Taft Benson explained that "the sacred mission of the Church . . . [is] to 'invite all to come unto Christ' (D&C 20:59)" ("'Come unto Christ,'" 84; see also Moroni 10:32). The law of sacrifice has always been a means for God's children to come unto the Lord Jesus Christ.

No one will ever accept the Savior without having faith in Him first. Hence, the first principle of the gospel is faith in the Lord Jesus Christ. Early leaders of the Church explained an important relationship between the principle of faith and the principle of sacrifice:

> Let us here observe, that three things are necessary in order that any rational and intelligent being may exercise faith in God. . . .

First, the idea that he actually exists.

Secondly, a *correct* idea of his character, perfections, and attributes.

Thirdly, an actual knowledge that the course of life which he is pursuing is according to his will. (*Lectures on Faith,* 38)

They then explained:

Let us here observe, that a religion that does not require the sacrifice of all things never has power sufficient to produce the faith necessary unto life and salvation. . . . It is through the medium of the sacrifice of all earthly things that men do actually know that they are doing the things that are well pleasing in the sight of God. When a man has offered in sacrifice all that he has for the truth's sake, not even withholding his life, and believing before God that he has been called to make this sacrifice because he seeks to do his will, he does know, most assuredly, that God does and will accept his sacrifice and offering, and that he has not, nor will not seek his face in vain. Under these circumstances, then, he can obtain the faith necessary for him to lay hold on eternal life. (*Lectures on Faith,* 69)

Let me summarize: To have faith and come unto Christ, we must know that God exists, have a correct understanding of God, know that what we do is pleasing before God, and understand that this knowledge comes to us through sacrifice and obedience. To those who come unto Christ in this way comes a confidence that whispers peace to their souls and that will eventually enable them to lay hold on eternal life.

I know—as I know that I live—that He lives. That is my testimony; and . . . I esteem it the highest honor that could be given to a man, to be a special witness of the Lord Jesus Christ. I hope you will be patient with me, and I shall do my best to come up to all the requirements the Lord will make at my hands.

—Melvin J. Ballard

Sacrifice allows us to learn something about ourselves—what we are willing to offer to the Lord through our obedience. To illustrate, Truman G. Madsen tells about a visit he made to Israel with President Hugh B. Brown. As they approached a valley known as Hebron, where tradition has it that there is a tomb of Father Abraham, Brother Madsen asked President Brown, "What are the blessings of Abraham, Isaac, and Jacob?"

After a short moment of thought, Elder Brown answered, "Posterity."

Brother Madsen wrote: "I almost burst out, 'Why, then, was Abraham commanded to go to Mount Moriah and offer his only hope of posterity?'

"It was clear that this man [President Brown], nearly ninety, had thought and prayed and wept over that question before. He finally said, 'Abraham needed to learn something about Abraham'" (Truman G. Madsen, *The Highest in Us,* 49).

> *I think as I read the story of Abraham's sacrifice of his son Isaac that our Father is trying to tell us what it cost Him to give His Son as a gift to the world.*
>
> —Melvin J. Ballard

Now let's look at another way that the law of sacrifice brought people unto Christ. Anciently, through blood sacrifices, the law of sacrifice brought people to Christ through typifying and foreshadowing His life and mission. Adam was taught that sacrifice was done as a "similitude of the sacrifice of the Only Begotten of the Father" (Moses 5:7). This teaches us that originally, ancient Israel understood the relationship between the sacrifice of their offerings and the sacrifice of the Lamb of God (see Doctrine and Covenants 138:12–13).

It is within the Book of Mormon that we find the clearest doctrinal teachings about the purpose of the law of sacrifice as practiced in the law of Moses. Nephi taught that sacrifice was done in remembrance of Christ (see 2 Nephi 11:4). He also stated:

"We keep the law of Moses, and look forward with steadfastness unto Christ. . . . For, for this end was the law given" (2 Nephi 25:24–25).

Amulek testified that Christ's ultimate sacrifice was "the whole meaning of the law, every whit pointing to that great and last sacrifice" (Alma 34:14).

And in Alma we read: "They did look forward to the coming of Christ, considering that the law of Moses was a type of his coming. . . . The law of Moses did serve to strengthen their faith in Christ" (Alma 25:15–16).

The Prophet Joseph Smith taught, "Whenever the Lord revealed Himself to men in ancient days, and commanded them to offer sacrifice to Him, . . . it was done that they might look forward in faith to the time of His coming, and rely upon the power of that atonement for a remission of their sins" (*Teachings of the Prophet Joseph Smith,* 60–61; see also 58).

Elder Russell M. Nelson taught: "We are still commanded to sacrifice, but not by shedding blood of animals. Our highest sense of sacrifice is achieved as we make ourselves more sacred or holy. This we do by our obedience to the commandments of God. Thus, the laws of obedience and sacrifice are indelibly intertwined. . . . As we comply with these and other commandments, something wonderful happens to us. . . . We become more sacred and holy—[more] like our Lord!" ("Lessons from Eve," 88).

> *Ought we not to rejoice in the testimony of the truth, and ought we not to give glory to God? After He has done so much for us, ought we not to do all we can for Him, and for His children all over the world, no matter who they are, where they are, or what they are? . . . God has done so much for us that if we do all we can and live to the age of a tree, we will never be able to repay Him for his goodness to us.*
>
> —Hyrum Mack Smith

It is interesting to note that the word *sacrifice* means literally "to make sacred" or "to render sacred."

The purposes of the law of sacrifice are eternal. The ways it has been practiced, however, have varied according to the Lord's will.

THE LAW OF SACRIFICE IN THE PREMORTAL LIFE

Our first lessons about the law of sacrifice, along with an understanding of all gospel principles, began in our premortal life. In the premortal world, we were taught the fulness of the gospel and the plan of salvation (see Doctrine and Covenants 138:56). We knew of the Savior's mission and of His future atoning sacrifice, and we willingly sustained Him as our Savior and our Redeemer. In fact, we learn from Revelation 12:11 that it is by "the blood of the Lamb" (Christ's atoning sacrifice) and our testimony that we are able to overcome Satan. President Joseph F. Smith explained:

> *In the very beginning, when the Lord desired to know whom He should send to represent Him here in the earth, who offered themselves? Two glorious sons of God. One was accepted and the other was rejected, and the one who was rejected rebelled and was disobedient.*
>
> —Melvin J. Ballard

> The Lord designed in the beginning to place before man the knowledge of good and evil, and gave him a commandment to cleave to good and abstain from evil. But if he should fail, he would give to him the law of sacrifice and provide a Savior for him, that he might be brought back again into the presence and favor of God and partake of eternal life with him. This was the plan of redemption chosen and instituted by the Almighty before man was placed on the earth. (*Gospel Doctrine*, 202)

THE LAW OF SACRIFICE FROM ADAM TO THE PROPHET MOSES

Adam and Eve were given the law of sacrifice and commanded to practice it by giving offerings. These included two emblems: the firstlings of the flock and the first fruits of the field. They obeyed without questioning (see Moses 5:5–6). President David O. McKay explained, "The effect of this [law] was that the best the earth produced, the best specimen in the flock or herd should not be used for self, but for God" ("The Atonement," 66). At a time in history when a primary concern was just making sure your family had food, those who sought to worship the Lord were asked to sacrifice the best part of their source of life. It was a real test of Adam and Eve's faith, and they obeyed.

Likewise, Abel, Noah, Abraham, Isaac, Jacob, and all the holy prophets from Adam to Moses offered the Lord sacrifices in a similar way.

THE LAW OF SACRIFICE FROM MOSES TO THE END OF CHRIST'S LIFE

Because of the rebellious nature of the children of Israel in the days of Moses, the law of sacrifice changed and became a strict law requiring a daily practice of performances and ordinances. From Adam's day to Moses's, there was just one kind of sacrifice offered. During the time of Moses, there was an expansion in the number and variety of offerings under the law of sacrifice. A detailed explanation of the varieties and degrees of sacrifices is far less important than an understanding of their purpose. The real value in understanding these offerings is that by so doing, we learn more about Jesus Christ, His infinite atoning sacrifice, and what we must do to come unto Him.

> *The children of Israel had the law of the gospel, but they could not live up to it, and so the law of Moses was given. That was all they could live by. That was a small part of the law of Christ.*
> —Melvin J. Ballard

While there were many different offerings, one thing remained the same in all of them. Everything about Mosaic sacrifice focused on Christ. Like Christ, the priest acted as the mediator between the people and their God. Like Christ, the priest had to have the right parentage to officiate in his office. Like Christ, the offerer through obedience willingly sacrificed what was required by the law. The part of sacrifice that most strongly paralleled the Savior was the offering itself. Notice with me some of these parallels.

> *In the time of Moses the Lord gave commandments to Israel, in which He told them they were to worship the Lord God, and none else. They were not to make unto themselves any other gods, nor bow down to the likenesses of anything in the heavens or in the earth; but Him only were they to worship.*
> —Hyrum Mack Smith

First, like Christ, the animal was chosen and anointed by the laying on of hands. The Hebrew name *Messiah* and the Greek name *Christ* both mean "the Anointed One." Second, the animal spilt its life's blood. Third, it had to be without blemish—totally free from physical flaws, complete, whole, and perfect. Fourth, the sacrifice had to be domesticated, that is—not wild but tame and of help to man (see Leviticus 1:2–3, 10; 22:21; Numbers 15:3). Sixth and seventh, for the original sacrifice practiced by Adam and the most common sacrifice in the law of Moses, the animal had to be a firstborn and a male (see Exodus 12:5; Leviticus 1:3; 22:18–25). Eighth, the sacrifice of grain had to be ground into flour and made into breadstuffs, which reminds us of our Lord's title, "the Bread of Life" (see John 6:48). Ninth, the first fruits that were offered remind us that Christ was the first fruits of the Resurrection (see 1 Corinthians 15:20). The Savior truly was the focus and purpose of each sacrifice.

THE LAW OF SACRIFICE IN THE NEW TESTAMENT AND A FULFILLMENT OF THE LAW OF MOSES

The law of sacrifice and the system of offerings as given to Moses continued to be practiced in New Testament times. Because

Jesus Christ of the New Testament was Jehovah of the Old Testament, it is He who gave the law of Moses in the first place. It would seem only appropriate, then, that He would be the one with authority to fulfill that law.

Jehovah in Old Testament times knew the details of His future atoning sacrifice and, therefore, prescribed elements of the law of Moses that specifically pointed to it. Then, with His final words, "It is finished" (John 19:30), the Lord pronounced the fulfillment of the law of Moses. Amulek spoke of the fulfillment of the law in this way:

> Therefore, it is expedient that there should be a great and last sacrifice, and then shall there be . . . a stop to the shedding of blood; then shall the law of Moses be fulfilled. . . .
>
> And behold, this is the whole meaning of the law, every whit pointing to that great and last sacrifice; and that great and last sacrifice will be the Son of God, yea, infinite and eternal. (Alma 34:13–14)

I stand as a special witness of this most singular event of all time. I testify in a unique way of the far-reaching effects of this most holy of all offerings. In a future day of another life when our finite reasoning will be expanded, we will more fully understand the penetrating powers of the Atonement and feel moved even more with gratitude, admiration, worship, and love toward our Savior in ways not possible in this present state.

When I think of this offering of Jesus Christ, in that he took upon himself the sins of the world, I cannot think of it and stand aloof from it not a participator; neither do I think that men [and women] can properly comprehend the mission of Jesus Christ who merely are interested in reading the story and are onlookers. Every man and woman who lives must be participators in this great sacrifice, if they are to be benefactors of that great atoning offering of the Lord Jesus Christ.

—Melvin J. Ballard

> *When this sacrifice which Christ required of the members of the Church seemed to be increasing, some began to chafe under it. Many had been accustomed to the old Jewish rituals; their hearts were not pure. But the spirit of many, even in that day, was that by some one act or some one service they might obtain the coveted goal of salvation or exaltation, and when Jesus made His requirements which seemed to be rather burdensome, some began to fall away.*
> —Melvin J. Ballard

At the fulfillment of the law of Moses, the Lord changed the practice of the law of sacrifice. To change a law that had been practiced for centuries served as a means to further emphasize the importance of the Atonement. Prior to the Atonement, blood sacrifice pointed forward to His sacrifice; after the Atonement, the sacrament points minds back to the Atonement.

The law of Moses is not the same thing as the law of sacrifice. Although the law of Moses was fulfilled, the principles of the law of sacrifice continue to be a part of the doctrine of the Church.

Although the primary purpose of the law of sacrifice continued to be that of testing us and assisting us to come unto Christ, two adjustments were made after Christ's ultimate sacrifice. First, the ordinance of the sacrament replaced the ordinance of blood sacrifice; and second, this change moved the focus of the sacrifice from a person's animal to the person. In a sense, the sacrifice changed from the offering to the offerer.

SACRIFICE VERSUS SACRAMENT

As we contemplate the replacing of animal sacrifice with the sacrament, we cannot help but notice a strong relationship between the two. Both sacrifice and sacrament:

- Are affected by a person's attitude and worthiness (see Amos 5:21–22; 3 Nephi 18:27–29; Moroni 7:6–7).
- Were designed to be performed by priests officiating in

the Aaronic Priesthood (see Doctrine and Covenants 13:1; 20:46).

- Focus on Christ (see Luke 22:19–20; Alma 34:13–14)
- Contain emblems that represent Christ's flesh and blood (see Luke 22:19–20; Moses 5:7).
- Provide a means whereby we can make and renew covenants with God (see Leviticus 22:21; Doctrine and Covenants 20:77–79).
- Are performed regularly on the Sabbath as well as on other special occasions (see Leviticus 23:15; Doctrine and Covenants 59:9–13).
- Are associated with meals that symbolically partake of the Atonement (see Leviticus 7:18; Matthew 26:26).
- Share the distinction that they're the only saving ordinance in which members participate for themselves more than once.
- Provide an important step in the process of repentance (see Leviticus 19:22; 3 Nephi 18:11; Moses 5:8).

The sacred covenant of the sacrament with its attendant blessings, which we repeat as we consecrate the emblems of the broken body and the spilt blood of the Lord, has been especially revealed to the Latter-day Saints by the Lord Himself. . . . By the act of partaking of the bread and the water, we make a solemn covenant that we do take upon us the name of our Redeemer, and that we do, further, make a pledge and an agreement by that act that we will keep His commandments.

—Melvin J. Ballard

President Joseph F. Smith compared the purpose of the sacrament with ancient sacrifice when he said that the purpose of the sacrament "is that we may keep in mind continually the Son of God who has redeemed us from eternal death, and brought us to life again through the power of the gospel. Before the coming of Christ to the earth, this was borne in mind . . . by another ordinance [blood sacrifice] which was a type of the great sacrifice that should take place in the meridian of time" (*Gospel Doctrine,* 103).

THE SACRIFICE OF OURSELVES INSTEAD OF OUR ANIMALS

After His mortal ministry, Christ elevated the law of sacrifice to a new level. In describing how the law of sacrifice would continue, Jesus told His Nephite Apostles that He would no longer accept burnt offerings but that His disciples should offer "a broken heart and a contrite spirit" (3 Nephi 9:19–20; see also Doctrine and Covenants 59:8, 12). Instead of the Lord requiring a person's animal or grain, now the Lord wants us to give up all that is ungodly. This is a higher practice of the law of sacrifice; it reaches into the inner soul of a person. Elder Neal A. Maxwell described it this way: "Real, personal sacrifice never was placing an animal on the altar. Instead, it is a willingness to put the animal in us upon the altar and letting it be consumed!" ("'Deny Yourselves,'" 68).

> *The religion of the Savior—and there is no other genuine Christianity—is, in its essence, to love God more than any other object of affection, and to love our fellowmen as we love ourselves.*
> —Hyrum Mack Smith

How is it that we show the Lord we have symbolically put ourselves upon today's sacrificial altar? We show the Lord we are willing to live the law of sacrifice today by living the first great commandment. Jesus said: "Thou shalt love the Lord thy God with all thy heart, and with all thy soul, and with all thy mind. This is the first and great commandment" (Matthew 22:37–38).

When we overcome our own selfish desires and put God first in our lives and covenant to serve Him regardless of the cost, then we are living the law of sacrifice. One of the best ways to keep the first great commandment is to keep the second great commandment. The Master Himself taught that "inasmuch as ye have done it unto one of the least of these my brethren, ye have done it unto me" (Matthew 25:40) and that "when ye are in the service of your fellow beings ye are only in the service of your God" (Mosiah 2:17). Sacrifice is a demonstration of pure love. The degree of our love for the Lord and for others can be measured by what we are willing to sacrifice for them.

> *There is no such thing as love without sacrifice and service. And those who sacrificed most and serve best love most.*
> —Melvin J. Ballard

Today in the Church, there are many examples of sacrifice that may help us understand that sacrifice for the gospel is not over and that coming unto Christ requires as much commitment and devotion today as it ever has.

Some time ago, I was assigned to preside over a regional conference in La Paz, Bolivia. Members came to the conference from small towns and villages scattered throughout the area of La Paz and the Altiplano. Great sacrifice and commitment were required of some of these members to attend the meetings. Prior to the priesthood leadership training session, I stood in front of the stake center and greeted the brethren as they gathered. I greeted one older brother who told me that he lived a long way from La Paz. I noticed that his shirt was a different color from the middle of his chest down. The upper portion of his shirt was white, whereas the lower portion was a brownish-red color.

I learned that he and three of his companions, all Melchizedek Priesthood holders, had taken many hours to travel to the meeting. They had walked most of the way and had to ford two rivers where the brownish-red water came up to their chests. They had flagged down a truck and stood in the back of it for the last two hours of their journey to the stake center.

This faithful man said to me: "Elder Ballard, you are one of the Lord's Apostles. My brethren and I would do whatever was required to be taught by you." Imagine how humble that made me feel. Do we have a similar attitude when we are asked to attend leadership meetings in our wards or stakes?

THE BLESSINGS OF SACRIFICE

We sing, "Sacrifice brings forth the blessings of heaven" ("Praise to the Man," *Hymns,* no. 27). This is a true principle. Let me illustrate:

I was named bishop of the Holladay Twelfth Ward in 1958. In those days, local members paid 50 percent of the cost of constructing a building. One of the most important leadership experiences in my life came several weeks before the announced dedication of the building we were constructing. Our ward of young families, who were struggling to make ends meet, needed to raise the final $30,000 to pay for our share of the cost. I fasted and prayed to know what I should say to our ward members regarding this obligation. We already had pressed them very hard, and they had willingly contributed money and personal labor beyond anything I believed possible, but still we needed to raise the last $30,000.

As the brethren gathered for priesthood meeting, I was impressed to read to them the testimony my Grandfather Ballard bore when he was ordained to the Quorum of the Twelve Apostles on January 7, 1919. In it, he spoke of a wonderful manifestation he had received in answer to sincere prayers about problems they were having in the work of the kingdom. He bore a strong personal testimony of the love of our Savior and Redeemer, Jesus Christ.

At the conclusion of this testimony, the Spirit of the Lord touched our hearts. Very little else was said because this small group of faithful brethren in the priesthood meeting also knew in their own way that Jesus Christ is the Son of God and that He is our Savior and Redeemer. We all knew that with greater faith in Him, we could reach our goal. During that same day, family after family came to my office with money, making personal sacrifices that were far beyond what I, the bishop, would ever have asked of them. By eight o'clock Sunday evening, the ward clerk had written receipts for a little more than $30,000.

Sacrifice truly brought forth the blessings of heaven to the members of our ward. Never have I lived among a people who were more united, more caring, and more concerned for one another than these ward members were. In the midst of our greatest sacrifice, we became bonded together in the true spirit of the gospel of love and service.

Today, the budget allowance procedures have lifted much of the financial sacrifice. Yet sacrifice is still necessary if we are to develop faith strong enough to lay hold on eternal life. I believe we should increase our spiritual devotion and service to the Lord and others to demonstrate to the Lord our love for Him and our Heavenly Father.

> *I saw, seated on a raised platform, the most glorious being I have ever conceived of, and was taken forward to be introduced to Him. . . . I fell at His feet, and there saw the marks of the nails; and as I kissed them, with deep joy swelling through my whole being, I felt that I was in heaven indeed. The feeling that came to my heart then was: Oh! If I could live worthy . . . so that in the end when I have finished I could go into His presence and receive the feeling that I then had in His presence, I would give everything that I am and ever hope to be!*
> —Melvin J. Ballard

THE CHALLENGE TO SACRIFICE

Today, we are not called to pull handcarts through the snow-swept plains of Wyoming. What we are asked to sacrifice may be different, but it may be just as difficult. Listen to the language of the scriptures as they describe the level of sacrifice the Lord requires of us: "Offer your whole souls as an offering unto [God]" (Omni 1:26; see also Mosiah 2:21). "Present your bodies a living sacrifice, holy, acceptable unto God" (Romans 12:1). The Lord Himself said that we should keep our "covenants by sacrifice—yea, every sacrifice which I, the Lord, shall command" (Doctrine and Covenants 97:8). The sacrifice the Lord asks of us is to wholly rid ourselves of the "natural man" and all the ungodliness associated with it (Mosiah 3:19). When we completely surrender ourselves to the Lord, then He will cause a mighty change in us; and we will become a new person, justified, sanctified, and born again with His image in our countenances (see Mosiah 5:2; Alma 5:14; Moses 6:59–60).

We must overcome the temptation to look upon our engagement in the Lord's vineyard as a sacrifice. . . . It is an honor and a privilege.
—Hyrum Mack Smith

As in all things, our Lord and Savior manifested the supreme example of sacrifice. His life and ministry established a pattern for us to follow. His divine mission was culminated in a supreme act of love as He gave His life for our redemption. Through His personal sacrifice, He provided a way for us to have our sins forgiven and return to the presence of our Father.

The principle of sacrifice is a law of God. We are obliged to understand it and to teach it and to practice it. If it becomes too easy to be a member of this Church, testimonies will become shallow; the roots of testimony will not go down into the soil like they did with our pioneer forefathers. May God grant you an understanding of the law of sacrifice and the conviction that it is with us today. It is vitally important that we understand it, teach it, and live it.

May your love for the Lord increase as you continue to

willingly serve Him. May the blessings that come from quiet sacrifice serve to strengthen your testimony and devotion to God.

This is His Church; He presides over it. He loves us and will guide us if we surrender our sins and our ungodliness and completely trust in Him.

CHAPTER 9

HAPPY TODAY

I SUPPOSE ALL OF US, at one time or another, find that our lives are not much like the lives we had imagined for ourselves in our youth. If you are now an adult, in all likelihood, your dreams at the age of fifteen or sixteen reflected a future far different from what you now experience. I know that when I was a teenager, I would never have imagined myself serving among the Apostles of the Lord Jesus Christ.

No matter our circumstances in life, we need to learn to be happy in the reality of today. What I will address here is the *how* of being happy no matter the challenges we face.

> *Our trust is in the Lord. Upon Him we depend, and we look in faith unto Him to give us strength and wisdom and the inspiration of the Holy Spirit to accomplish with success, and to His name's honor and glory, the work He has called us to do.*
> —HYRUM MACK SMITH

First, and most important, to be truly happy, we must "Trust in the Lord with all thine heart; and lean not unto thine own understanding" (Proverbs 3:5).

To trust in the Lord means that we know Him and have confidence that He loves us and understands what we are experiencing. We have faith in Him and in what He has done for us through the Atonement and Resurrection.

Remember the people of Alma who were in bondage to the Lamanites and were forbidden to pray at peril of death. They "did pour out their hearts to [God]; and he did know the thoughts of their hearts."

> And it came to pass that the voice of the Lord came to them in their afflictions, saying: Lift up your heads and be of good comfort, . . . [and] I will also ease the burdens which are put upon your shoulders. . . .
>
> And now it came to pass that the burdens which were laid upon Alma and his brethren were made light; yea, *the Lord did strengthen them that they could bear up their burdens with ease,* and they did submit cheerfully and with patience to all the will of the Lord. (Mosiah 24:12–15; emphasis added)

The Lord didn't remove the burdens or the challenges, but He strengthened the people to enable them to handle the burdens with ease—and with cheerfulness and patience.

I would like to encourage you with all the strength of my soul to work to build a real, personal relationship with the Savior of the world. I do not know of anything that is more important than to know you are in tune with Him. It takes fasting, it takes mighty prayer, it takes diligent and committed service, it takes searching and pondering the scriptures, and it takes obedience to His commandments.

It is not only important that we shall know how to pray, but it is equally important that we shall know how to receive the answer to our prayer, to be discerning, to be alert, to be able to see with clear vision and understand with clear intention God's will and purpose concerning us.
—Melvin J. Ballard

As you pray, I encourage you to think in terms of whom you are addressing. Be prepared in every way to build your communication with your Heavenly Father, to be entitled to the inspiration of the Holy Ghost.

May I tell you of a special experience I had some years ago that conveys what I am trying to encourage you to understand. Shortly after I was called to the First Quorum of the Seventy, I went back to my mission in Toronto, Canada—that was in April of 1976—and in May, the next month, we held a solemn assembly in eastern Canada for all the priesthood leaders. The First Presidency, one of the Twelve, and one of the Assistants to the Twelve came at that time to hold that solemn assembly. It was a glorious experience. I was the chairman because I was then among the newest General Authorities of the Church.

> *Prophets have been raised up who speak with the same peculiar power, inspiration, and authority as the prophets of old.*
> —Hyrum Mack Smith

At the end of the solemn assembly, we had a light dinner for the Brethren, and then I drove the First Presidency back to the hotel where they were staying. When we arrived at the hotel, the Brethren bade me good night and went to the ninth floor. Then I noticed that President Spencer W. Kimball's secretary, Arthur Haycock, had been detained at the counter, so I went over and asked him if I could take the key up to President Kimball so that he might get into his room. He appreciated my offering to do that and handed me the key. I took the elevator to the ninth floor and went down the hall. There I saw President N. Eldon Tanner and President Kimball standing in the doorway. As I approached them, I said, "President, here is your key. I thought I'd bring it up to you so you could get in and have a good night's rest."

He thanked me for that in his loving way, and then President Tanner took my arm and asked, "Russ, would you like to come in and have prayer with us?" Can you imagine the impact on me in closing the day with the First Presidency of the Church? I went into President Tanner's room with President Kimball. It was but a moment before President Marion G. Romney and the other Brethren came in. I was overwhelmed. Tears welled up in my eyes as we knelt down around President Tanner's bed.

I was kneeling next to President Tanner when President

Kimball said, "Eldon, this is your room. Whom would you like to have pray?" I think President Tanner sensed what was happening to me, for he said, "President, we would like you to pray." And then I heard our dear prophet pray. I learned a great lesson from that simple, humble prayer. I felt the Spirit as I had never felt it before as I listened to a prophet talk to God. It seemed like two close friends speaking to each other.

What the Latter-day Saints are living for and hoping for . . . is the word we expect to hear when we go before the Master, our God and Father; that when He shall look into our hearts He can say, "Well done, thou good and faithful servant." That will be the happiest and the most glorious thing that [we] can ever hear. That is what we are living for, and to have achieved it is to have accomplished success—success in life, and salvation.

—Hyrum Mack Smith

It was a short but powerful prayer. President Kimball prayed, "Heavenly Father, we pray above everything else we have done that the labors of this day have been acceptable unto Thee." That penetrated my heart like nothing else ever has on the principle of prayer. Oh, that every one of us might always be found closing the day pleading that our lives have been acceptable unto God that day! There is great strength in knowing that God is our Father, that we are His sons and daughters, and that He loves us as we strive to have our lives acceptable to Him.

As I left the room, President Kimball said, "We love you, Elder Ballard!" While waiting for the elevator, I had an overwhelming spiritual experience, reaffirming to me that I had knelt before God in the presence of His apostles and prophets.

Second, to be happy, we must study the life and teachings of Jesus Christ through the scriptures, and we must obey His gospel.

When I contemplate the Savior's birth in a manger because there was no room in the inn, along with the circumstances under which He grew up as a boy, I relate that to how I was born and grew up, and the differences seem grossly unfair. Somehow I feel that if anyone who was ever born into the world would be entitled to have the bounteous blessings of life, surely it would be the Son of God. Yet He came into this world in the lowliest of circumstances. As I read the scriptures about His life and try to understand Him, I can see that He rose above it all.

As I study the Savior's life, I see in Him a man who was so committed to His cause and His mission, whose eye was so single to the glory of our eternal Heavenly Father, that regardless of the circumstances or the pressures that came into His life, regardless of those who persecuted Him and reviled Him and tried to harm Him, He was somehow able to set all of that aside and see the good in every man and woman. Somehow He was always able to be on higher ground and able to reach down and lift those about Him to a higher level.

Every page, almost, of the holy scriptures bears record and attests the divinity of Christ. . . . So far as the Latter-day Saints are concerned, we know these things are true. There is no doubt in our minds about it. Why? Because the Spirit of Truth, the Holy Ghost, has been received by us.
—Hyrum Mack Smith

When I read of the last few days of His life upon the earth before His Resurrection, I consider how the people treated Him, how they reviled Him, spit upon Him, and took reeds and beat Him. I consider how they persecuted Him to the degree that they even thrust upon His back, in His weakened condition, His own cross and forced Him to carry it. When I read that He fell under the weight of that cross and could carry it no more, my love for Him grows stronger and deeper.

Do you love Jesus Christ so much that you can look heavenward and, regardless of what occurs in your life, be happy in the knowledge that He lives, that He is our Savior, our Redeemer, our Elder Brother, our God, who gave us the promise of the

Resurrection and eternal life? Without Him, we would have no eternal future. Because of Him, we have the hope of eternal life in His presence and in the presence of our Heavenly Father.

I know of no greater tribute you or I could give than to commit within our individual hearts that we will be better, that we will strive to be more like Him. If you have anything in your life that needs to be corrected and repented of, commit today that you will correct those things that sow seeds of doubt and frustration.

Through the years, I have had the opportunity to interview many people. I remember once feeling impressed as I interviewed a man to ask him to tell me how he felt about the Lord Jesus Christ. He talked to me about his feelings and seemed sincere in his expression.

I then said to him, "Would you do anything in this world that the Lord asked you to do?"

He said, "Oh yes."

"Would you give your life if necessary, if He called upon you to do it? Do you love Him that much?"

"Oh yes."

It is within the power of every one of us to repent of our sins, because the Lord is merciful, and the Lord is quick to forgive. But repentance means that we cease to sin when we discover that an act is sinful, and do it no more; that is repentance.
—Hyrum Mack Smith

I asked him about his feelings toward the Prophet Joseph Smith, and he briefly shared his testimony with me.

Then I asked him a very penetrating question, "Have you studied the scriptures and pondered and prayed about them, and do you know the Church is true?"

His eyes dropped, and then he raised them back up and said, "Well, I've read parts of the Book of Mormon; I feel good about Joseph Smith, and I feel good about the Church." But he could not say that he read from the Book of Mormon or from the other scriptures each day as the prophets have asked us to do. And his testimony was unsure and weak.

The counsel to you to study the scriptures each day, especially the Book of Mormon, comes because all too often the winds of life will blow against you. You will continue to be tested. That is the purpose of life. That is the reason we have been sent here, to determine just how committed and dedicated we really are. So the test will continue. But if you have a foundation built under you, an anchoring testimony of your own that Jesus Christ is the Son of God and our Redeemer, that Joseph Smith is a prophet of God, and that the gospel has been restored, you have nothing to fear. You will be prepared for whatever tests and challenges come into your life.

> *May the Lord teach us to be obedient, to be humble, to be peaceable, and to be faithful, to stand in this testing time, for this is a testing time, when individuals are being tested—no great assault against the Church, but a mighty assault on the part of the evil one against every individual.*
>
> —Melvin J. Ballard

Third, I emphasize service.

Sometimes, as challenges come, we start to question whether we are important in the grand scheme of things and whether our Heavenly Father loves us and has need of us in His kingdom.

Find ways to be of service. It can be as simple as a telephone call or a note to someone who is ill. Each of us needs to think outside ourselves if we are to be happy. In whatever calling yours might be, commit to do it better tomorrow than you have ever done it before.

A part of our service wherein we will find great joy is that of sharing our knowledge and testimony of the Savior and of the Restoration of His gospel to the earth through the Prophet Joseph Smith.

Two missionaries serving in the Deep South understood their

missionary purpose and the connection to the principle of genuine service.

Over a number of years, a local ward routinely had invited the city mayor to participate in open-house events and speak in a sacrament meeting. Sometimes the mayor accepted the invitations to attend open houses, generally held on a Saturday, but he always politely declined invitations to speak on a Sunday in the ward.

He easily recognized the missionaries—the young men who rode bikes but wore white shirts, ties, and helmets. Whenever they approached him, he routinely waved them on or politely declined an opportunity to visit.

Later, these two missionaries were riding down a residential street when they noticed the mayor and his wife remodeling a house. The missionaries later learned that the house was a rental property owned by the mayor and his wife. Seeing an opportunity to provide some service, the missionaries walked up to the front door to ask if they could help move a rather large roll of used carpet from the front lawn into a nearby truck.

> *Our labors when performed in faith and full purpose of heart, and with sincere desire, cannot be in vain. There must be a harvest, and it only remains for the harvesters to gather it.*
> —Hyrum Mack Smith

When the mayor greeted them, he told them firmly but politely that he was too busy to talk with them at that time. The missionaries responded by offering to help move the bulky carpet roll. Again, the mayor declined their offer and walked back into the house.

A few minutes later, he emerged from the house and found that the missionaries had taken off their helmets, picked up the heavy carpet roll, and were making their way to the pickup truck. The mayor and his wife were surprised but grateful for the help, as they knew they could not have moved the carpet by themselves.

The missionaries continued helping for about half an hour. When the work was done, the mayor and his wife invited the missionaries to enjoy a cold glass of water. During the short time they cordially visited with each other as a consequence of the missionaries' service, the mayor finally consented, after years of avoidance, to listen to what they had to say.

The missionaries shared the story of the Restoration with this couple, and the mayor and his wife were genuinely impressed by the power of the young men's testimonies, which equaled the physical strength they had exhibited when moving the huge carpet roll into the truck.

Because of the service they rendered and the beautiful message about Jesus Christ they shared, the missionaries made two friends that day; and the mayor and his wife were no longer inclined to wave the missionaries on as they had done for years.

As you might expect, the annual invitation to speak in a sacrament meeting was extended to the mayor shortly thereafter. This time, however, the mayor surprised the bishop by accepting the invitation to speak about community service in an upcoming sacrament meeting.

As a result of the turn of events, the bishop decided to invite the mission president to be the final speaker on that special occasion. Before the meeting began, the mayor shared with the mission president the story of the two bright, strong missionaries and commented that their service had softened his heart and had prompted him to listen to them and then to accept the invitation to speak in a Sunday meeting.

He confessed that he had declined in the past because he worried that voters might not appreciate his speaking in "that church" on a Sunday. However, after witnessing true Christian service from the missionaries, and after listening to their missionary message about Jesus Christ and His restored gospel, he pointed out that his prejudices of the past were dispelled.

The sacrament meeting went well and allowed the local Saints to hear their city mayor talk about community service, especially about ways they could make a difference through their service in the community. In turn, the mayor and his wife heard the Christ-centered sacramental prayers, listened to the beautiful music praising the Lord, made many new friends, and heard the mission president give a gospel-centered talk on service that was rooted in the scriptures.

Sometimes we forget to invite the Lord to direct us in our service to others through the power of the Holy Ghost. The Lord knows His sheep, for He is the Good Shepherd. I believe that He knows the honest in heart. He knows who needs your loving service.

> *We ought to rely a little more than we do upon the Lord and upon the intelligence He has given us to develop the light within us, to become better informed, to be more faithful than we are, notwithstanding good testimony of our faithfulness may be borne now.*
> —Hyrum Mack Smith

Fourth, share the gospel. How different the world is today from just a few years ago! There are so many more ways to share the gospel than there have ever been. The Lord over the centuries has had a hand in inspiring people to invent tools that facilitate the spreading of the gospel. There are perhaps few inventions that have had a greater impact on the world than the printing press, invented by Johannes Gutenberg in 1436. The printing press enabled knowledge, including the Holy Bible, to be shared more widely than ever before. Ultimately, the common people had access to the truths of scripture. The printing press played a major role in the Reformation and in the Restoration. Without the printing press, the Restoration would have been much more difficult.

Today, we have a modern equivalent of the printing press in

the Internet and all that it means. The Internet allows everyone to be a publisher, to have his or her voice heard, and it is revolutionizing society. Today, it is possible for nearly anyone to publish or broadcast to either a large or a niche audience. The emergence of new media is facilitating a worldwide conversation on almost every subject, including religion, and nearly everyone can participate.

> *Greater human progress has been made in the development of science in the last hundred years than in all the preceding ages combined. Surely the Spirit of God has been poured out upon all flesh, and men have caught visions of the secrets of God and the materialization of these visions has produced wonders in the heavens and upon the earth. The Lord's hand is in all that is now going forward.*
> —Melvin J. Ballard

I probably don't need to tell you that there is much questionable information, even outright falsehoods, about the Church on the Internet and in the media—much bad mixed with the good. So let me pose a question: What are *you* prepared to do about it? What is your responsibility? If a national conversation is going on about the Church, are you going to be an active participant or a silent observer? How can you use these marvelous inventions to help further the work of the Lord?

Church leaders can't do it all, especially at the grassroots, community level. Though we do speak authoritatively for the Church, we look to our responsible and faithful members to engage personally with blogs, to write thoughtful, online letters to news organizations, and to act in other ways to correct the record with their own opinions.

However, I emphasize that it is not always about correcting misinformation. Sometimes, it is about getting solid information and ideas out there in the first place. Share your experiences—those from your own life—that show how your values and your faith intersect. It doesn't matter whether that's face-to-face with another person or whether you do it by participating from your own blog or social media platform or by contributing to someone else's comments. Of course, you will be speaking as an individual member and not as an official representative of the Church. The most important thing is that you let people know that you are a Latter-day Saint and that your behavior and attitude always reflect the high standards of the Church and what is expected as a follower of the Lord Jesus Christ.

Clearly, in this context, I am not talking about declaring your testimony of faith in the traditional sense. Naturally, you can and should do that where the setting is appropriate and the audience is receptive, such as a Church meeting. Rather, I am talking about taking part in everyday conversations in an unforced way, where your values and your religious beliefs will arise naturally. People do not like to have religion thrust down their throats. Instead, allow people to see how your beliefs lift and shape your life for the better. How do your values encourage you to participate in civic affairs? How has your experience as a home or visiting teacher enlarged your compassion or care for the sick and needy? How has your Church life helped you to avoid such things as pornography and immorality? How has your experience in speaking in Church meetings helped you address large public groups? Where did you learn to respect and not to criticize other faiths? And so on.

In many of these conversations, you will be sharing common ground with people who will relate to your values. And as people sense that common ground, your relationship with them and their respect for you and for your faith will be enhanced. Even people who may disagree with you philosophically will often accept you more readily for your candid,

> *The leaven is working, and the people of the world are coming to see the truth. They are preaching many of the truths that we preach and which were not known to be true . . . when Joseph Smith introduced them.*
> —Hyrum Mack Smith

honest, and open observations about how your faith impacts your life. I have a great belief in the basic fairness of most all people. They respect honesty, not timidity. They relate to sincerity, not to pretended piety.

And so I ask you to share the gospel, to be more open about your Church membership and about your values. Jesus Christ, the Son of God and Redeemer of the world, taught us how to live. He spoke in parables. He once compared the good people of the earth to the leaven used in baking bread. A little leaven raises the whole loaf, He said. At another time, He compared His followers to salt. If the salt loses its savor, "it is thenceforth good for nothing" but to be cast away and trodden underfoot (Matthew 5:13). Translate that into today's world, and we can see the parallel. Without being self-righteous or overbearing, we should allow our belief in the basic decency and goodness of humanity to shine through.

> *God help us to be loyal to each other, loyal to the cause, obedient to the counsels of those whom God calls to direct us; and the enemy who has sought to destroy us shall be no more successful in new methods than he was through bonds and imprisonment and mob violence.*
>
> —Melvin J. Ballard

Both the Apostle Paul and Joseph Smith taught that if there is anything lovely, of good report, or praiseworthy, we should seek after these things. The phrase "seeking after" suggests active participation, not passive acceptance. We should be active in our communities. We should join groups where we can exert a positive influence. We should embrace those who have similar values and try to better understand those who don't. We should join the conversations on the Internet or anywhere else where we can clarify the great purpose of God in restoring to the earth the fulness of the gospel of Jesus Christ through the Prophet Joseph Smith.

May the Lord bless us to find happiness today and joy in this life through our faith and trust in Him and our Heavenly Father, through our love for Him and His gospel generated by our personal study and prayer, and through our service to others.

CHAPTER 10

Trials Can Strengthen Our Faith

PRESIDENT JOHN TAYLOR made a profound statement over a hundred years ago that I have pondered many times:

> We are not here to follow the devices and desires of our own hearts; we are not here to carry out any particular theory of our own; we are not here to build up any system of man's creation; but we are here simply to do the will of God in the establishment of his kingdom on the earth. In many things however we have not lived up to that high and glorious privilege which has been presented to us; we have been careless and indifferent, and it seems as though Satan has been permitted to try and tempt us in every possible way. For a few years past a spirit of greed and covetousness has run through the land and cursed as with a withering blight every thing it has touched. It is as bad in its effects upon the mind of man as any pestilence or plague upon the human body. We have begun to run after the things of the world; our hearts, feelings and affections, in many instances, have been estranged from God. It is time that something should transpire to wake us up to a sense of the position we occupy; it is time we realized how God and angels look upon men who are absorbed in the things of this world instead of living up to their professions and the covenants they have made with him. (*Journal of Discourses,* 21:3)

Now, I suppose ever since Adam and Eve walked out of the Garden, men and women have struggled in trying to keep things in balance and trying to keep the spiritual side of life in focus and in proper view. I remind all of us that we are the sons and daughters of God. We have a concept about that that is unique to the Restoration of the gospel of Jesus Christ in these latter days. Inside each of our bodies is a spirit that is begotten of God, our Eternal Father. It was just a few moments ago, really, that we were living with our Heavenly Father and our Heavenly Mother in the great world of the spirits. We understand our premortal life because we have a prophet. Through the Prophet Joseph Smith, we have an understanding of the relationship we enjoy as the sons and daughters of God. We have come to this earth for a very important and significant purpose.

> *It is said that actions speak louder than words. If that is true, we do seem to have a difference of opinion as to the purposes of life. For some of us are spending our time and efforts, night and day, struggling forward through the years, in the accumulation of this world's goods. Others are spending themselves in the development of their personal talents, to bring upon themselves the credit and applause of the world. In fact, men and women by their actions are telling a different story as to the real purpose of life, so far as they are concerned.*
>
> —MELVIN J. BALLARD

This body of flesh and bones, this tabernacle that houses the spirit that was begotten of our Father, is a very important part of our eternal progression. We have to have this physical body to accomplish the everlasting and eternal prospects of our celestial exaltation in the presence of the Father and the Son. We have to have this capacity that a physical body gives us to become like God and to receive all the blessings that our Heavenly Father has for His children. The great quest, then, the great challenge that we face in mortality, is to work on the inner self, to work on the spiritual side of our nature.

I have often thought, and particularly I thought it as a mission president, how wonderful it would be if we could have a hunger and a thirst for the things of the Spirit that would be with us as regularly as our hunger and thirst for the things of the physical tabernacle. We like to get up in the morning and have breakfast; we like to have lunch; we like to have dinner; I knew some missionaries who liked to eat all the time. The food we take into our bodies is temporal, or physical, and it nourishes the temporal, physical side of us and gives us strength and energy so we can take on the battles of the day. It helps us get up and go and learn the things we need to learn in the process of this experience in mortality.

> *We eat food to stimulate our physical bodies. Without the partaking of food we would become weak and sickly, and fail physically. It is just as necessary, for our spiritual body, that we should partake of [the] sacrament and by it obtain spiritual food for our souls.*
> —Melvin J. Ballard

What a wonderful thing it would be if, on a regular basis, we could have the same craving for the things of the Spirit. You see, the everlasting part of you and me is the spiritual side of our being. The spirit will never die. The day will come when each one of us will die. What happens when somebody dies? We might say that he had a heart attack or she died of cancer or they died of this reason or that reason. But the moment of death really occurs when the spirit leaves the body and goes back to our Heavenly Father to wait for the season of the Resurrection. Oh, how important it is for us to focus our lives and take time in the process of going through this mortal experience to study the things of the Spirit, to build the inner self.

I will tell you a story that brought this to my mind in a most vivid way some years ago. Sister Ballard and I were in Brazil. There was a fireside in the evening with the young adults. I went to that fireside and spoke to them. I noticed particularly a young sister who was sitting in a wheelchair, disabled and terribly crippled by multiple sclerosis. For some reason, I felt a bonding with her as I was teaching. That happens on occasion; spirit to spirit you have a connection. At the conclusion of what I had to say, I went down and knelt on one knee and took hold of her hand so I could look her in the eye. It was difficult for her to hold her head up. I had an interpreter because she spoke only Portuguese. And she said to me these words, "Brother Ballard, why would God do this to me if He loves me? Why am I so ugly and so incapable of getting along in mortality?"

Tough questions! I looked at her face and into her eyes and said, "You know, there is something about you that is absolutely beautiful. I want you to understand that the real you is radiating a beautiful spirit. Don't you ever lose that. Don't curse God because of the challenges you have. Rather, let this wonderful spirit, captured inside this crippled body, soar. Let it touch as many lives as you know how to possibly do as you experience mortality. That glorious day will come when you will be relieved from this challenge in mortality; and I promise you in the name of the Lord that if you will work on the inner self, the real you, that you will have a sense of accomplishment, a sense of peace, a sense of joy that will be eternal in its nature."

I shall never forget how she looked back at me and said, "Do you really think I am beautiful?"

Did we know that [mortality] meant pain and sorrow and ultimately death? We knew all of that. But there was no power or influence to deter us from coming. We were eager to come.
—Melvin J. Ballard

And I replied, "Absolutely." I had really seen her beautiful spirit radiating through her eyes. All of us are the sons and daughters of God, and our spirits are equally as beautiful as her spirit.

When we talk about being ourselves, we are talking about our spirits—the inner person—the real person. As we love the Lord and keep His commandments, our spirits become even more glorious and refined.

Questions: Why do we have challenges? Why do we have trials? Why do we have to suffer? Why do we have difficulties in life? Part of the answer is that opposition is essential for us to learn to become like God and like His Beloved Son. Elder Orson F. Whitney taught:

> No pain that we suffer, no trial that we experience is wasted. It ministers to our education, to the development of such qualities as patience, faith, fortitude, and humility. All that we suffer and all that we endure, especially when we endure it patiently, builds up our characters, purifies our hearts, expands our souls, and makes us more tender and charitable, more worthy to be called the children of God. . . . And it is through sorrow and suffering, toil and tribulation, that we gain the education that we come here to acquire and which will make us more like our Father and Mother in heaven. (As quoted in Kimball, *Faith Precedes the Miracle,* 98)

It is the mortal body that dies, not the immortal spirit.
—Hyrum Mack Smith

In any given congregation of the Saints, there are some who are carrying particularly difficult trials and tribulations, some who are suffering. Perhaps you struggle with health problems that are difficult and that cause you to be anxious. Carry the burden well. Learn from your trials and tribulations those things that are uniquely important for you to learn as they pertain to the spiritual development of the real you.

Maybe you are among those who have lost their companions. Carry your loneliness, carry your challenge, with great dignity and power. Let your spiritual education reach out and touch and bless the lives of all those around you. Help them learn from their exposure to you that through trial and tribulation and suffering come spiritual strength and preparation for great things that yet lie ahead.

Many in our world are raising children alone as single mothers or fathers. There are those around you to whom you can turn for help—your bishop, your home and visiting teachers, the elders quorum presidency, high priests group leadership, and the Relief Society presidency. But I say to you, grow spiritually in the process. "Brother Ballard," you may say, "it is so hard." Life does have some very hard times and some very hard moments, and none of us is exempt from challenges in the process of getting through it. Listen to these words of Brigham Young: "You all know that the Saints must be made pure, to enter into the celestial kingdom. It is recorded that Jesus was made perfect through suffering. If he was made perfect through suffering, why should we imagine for one moment that we can be prepared to enter into the kingdom of rest with him and the Father, without passing through similar ordeals?" (*Journal of Discourses,* 8:66).

Why does the Lord permit us to suffer while in the body? Does that have any part in the divine plan? We never know joy until we have tasted sorrow. . . . To live in a mortal body full of pain, of sorrow, decrepitude and ultimately death, is all a preparation to make one understand what it means when the day shall come that death is swallowed up, that the grave will be no longer part of [our] experiences.
—MELVIN J. BALLARD

When I think of suffering, I think of some words that almost cause me to want to weep. From December 1838 through April 1839, the Prophet Joseph Smith, along with my great-great-grandfather Hyrum and others, was incarcerated in the Liberty Jail. Five long months! I have been to Liberty and have seen the jail and contemplated the horrible circumstances the brethren were in on dirt floors, ceilings so low that Joseph and

We do not wish our children to grow up with the feeling that all they ask of the Father shall be given them, for if all we ask were given us, it might prove our undoing and bring our destruction.
—Melvin J. Ballard

Hyrum couldn't stand up straight, rats running about, food that was not always tolerable, poor sanitation, and bitterly cold conditions. Finally, I suppose in exhaustion, Joseph cried out with these words:

> O God, where art thou? And where is the pavilion that covereth thy hiding place?
>
> How long shall thy hand be stayed, and thine eye, yea thy pure eye, behold from the eternal heavens the wrongs of thy people and of thy servants, and thine ear be penetrated with their cries?
>
> Yea, O Lord, how long shall they suffer these wrongs and unlawful oppressions, before thine heart shall be softened toward them, and thy bowels be moved with compassion toward them?
>
> O Lord God Almighty, maker of heaven, earth, and seas, and of all things that in them are, and who controllest and subjectest the devil, and the dark and benighted dominion of Sheol—stretch forth thy hand; let thine eye pierce; let thy pavilion be taken up; let thy hiding place no longer be covered; let thine ear be inclined; let thine heart be softened, and thy bowels moved with compassion toward us.
>
> Let thine anger be kindled against our enemies; and, in the fury of thine heart, with thy sword avenge us of our wrongs.
>
> Remember thy suffering saints, O our God; and thy servants will rejoice in thy name forever.

Then came this tender response from a loving, eternal Father:

> My son, peace be unto thy soul; thine adversity and thine afflictions shall be but a small moment;

> And then, if thou endure it well, God shall exalt thee on high; thou shalt triumph over all thy foes.
>
> Thy friends do stand by thee, and they shall hail thee again with warm hearts and friendly hands.
>
> Thou art not yet as Job; thy friends do not contend against thee, neither charge thee with transgression, as they did Job. (Doctrine and Covenants 121:1–10)

I don't know that the 121st section or the 122nd section of the Doctrine and Covenants could have come to the Prophet in any other way than by his preparation through suffering. You know the great declaration of the 121st section of the Doctrine and Covenants: When we are pressed up against the most difficult moments in our lives, that is when we have a spiritual insight, when we see things in the big picture, the eternal scheme of things, that we have never before been able to see.

Joseph F. Smith received one of the greatest revelations, in my judgment, that we have in the Church. I will tell you a little background to that revelation, which I know because of my relationship to Joseph F. Smith and to my grandfather Hyrum Mack Smith, who was his oldest son. I never knew my Grandfather Smith. In January 1918, ten years before I was born, he had a ruptured appendix, and with no penicillin available at that time, he died. I know from correspondence and from the writings in personal journals of Joseph F. Smith that the loss of his son Hyrum was a tremendously

How often do parents have to deny the prayers and petitions of their own children? Notwithstanding the child desires a thing greatly, and can see no reason why he should not have it, yet in the greater wisdom of the parent his request is denied and the supposed blessing is withheld. But that is no evidence that the prayer was not considered by the parent; it is simply an evidence that the parent knows best when to give and when to withhold.

—HYRUM MACK SMITH

difficult experience for the President of the Church. The letters between President Smith and my grandfather, particularly those written when my grandfather presided over the European Mission of the Church, expressed an affection and bonding that are rarely seen in writing between a father and a son.

I believe that the experience of losing Hyrum Mack at age forty-five in January 1918 and then his daughter-in-law, my grandmother Ida Elizabeth Bowman, at the age of forty-six, eight months later in September 1918 was the final catalyst for Joseph F. Smith to ponder and think about the things of the Spirit and the great plan of salvation in a way that set the stage for this remarkable vision.

In that moment of His trial, God's trial, in His suffering and sacrifice, He has manifested His interest in us, His love for us that should live forever. . . . And this monument of God's enduring love for [us], that He suffered thus to give His Son, should endure forever.
—Melvin J. Ballard

His spiritual preparation for this great vision began with the death of his own father, Hyrum Smith, in 1844, when Joseph F. was only five years old, and the death of his beloved mother, Mary Fielding Smith, in 1852, when Joseph F. was only thirteen years old. They had been his examples, counselors, and guides. Joseph F.'s love for family and those relationships naturally caused him to think about them after they died. Additionally, Joseph F. buried a number of children throughout his life, causing him much pain and thoughtful consideration about the subject of the dead.

Then, in October 1918, he penned these words, his last gift to the Church and world as he died in November a few weeks later:

> On the third of October, in the year nineteen hundred and eighteen, I sat in my room pondering over the scriptures;

And reflecting upon the great atoning sacrifice that was made by the Son of God, for the redemption of the world;

And the great and wonderful love made manifest by the Father and the Son in the coming of the Redeemer into the world;

That through his atonement, and by obedience to the principles of the gospel, mankind might be saved.

While I was thus engaged, my mind reverted to the writings of the apostle Peter, to the primitive saints scattered abroad throughout Pontus, Galatia, Cappadocia, and other parts of Asia, where the gospel had been preached after the crucifixion of the Lord.

I opened the Bible and read the third and fourth chapters of the first epistle of Peter, and as I read I was greatly impressed. . . .

As I pondered over these things which are written, the eyes of my understanding were opened, and the Spirit of the Lord rested upon me, and I saw the hosts of the dead, both small and great.

And there were gathered together in one place an innumerable company of the spirits of the just, who had been faithful in the testimony of Jesus while they lived in mortality. (Doctrine and Covenants 138: 1–6, 11–12)

I live in the hope of the glorious resurrection, that I, with the faithful in Christ, may be permitted to come forth in the resurrection of the just, clothed with glory, immortality, and eternal life, and may God implant this faith in increasing ratio in my heart and in the hearts of all who take upon themselves the name of Christ the Lord.

—Hyrum Mack Smith

In the spirit of personal suffering, President Joseph F. Smith found a quiet place and with scriptures in hand sat pondering over where his son was. He meditated upon the great plan of redemption that has been given to the world through the Lord Jesus Christ. The veil was lifted from his eyes, and he saw things spiritually that he never would have been able to see had he not been prepared spiritually to receive them.

We all experience challenges in life. There are financial challenges for some. There are health challenges. There are faith challenges. There are family challenges. God bless us to understand that the real you, the real me, is the inner part, the spiritual part. I promise you in the name of the Lord that if you will face your trials, your tribulations, your sufferings, whatever they may be, allowing your spirit to be taught, strengthened, and fortified, you will be equal to the challenge. You will have the power to endure to the end with your testimony firm and strong and powerful. Even in your anguish over your difficulties and your challenges, may the Lord bless you to set an example for your family, to set an example for the members of your ward, letting them know that you understand the gospel, that you understand that life in mortality is but a moment in time and that this suffering will pass quickly in relationship to eternity.

I confess that if I had the power to banish death I would not do it, for, after all, death is the kindest friend the human family has. What a world this would be if there were no death, with all the aged, the infirm, those full of pain and sorrow and distress! How we would be appalled to live in such a world!

—Melvin J. Ballard

May God bless us to really understand and know that we are, in fact, His children, that He does, in fact, love us, and that He will not let us suffer beyond our capacity to endure. In our challenges and in our quest in mortality, may we become strong spiritually.

Chances are you have met people in your life, as I have, who are filled with the Spirit. You come away from that meeting knowing you have never felt the power of the spirit of anyone quite like when you shook hands with this person or that person. As you meet such men or women, you feel something extraordinary. That is a great thing. It is a marvelous thing to be able to radiate an obedient, humble, submissive, willing spirit, one with ability to endure whatever life's challenge happens to be with a happy heart and with the positive, absolute assurance that it will be over soon. May we strive to be that kind of person. May we come to know that life will go on into the eternities where the Lord's promises to us will be fulfilled—every blessing that our Father in Heaven has for His faithful children will be given unto us. Not one blessing will be held back.

This is a great Church. We have great insight and knowledge available to us. We know the purpose of life beyond any other people on the face of the earth. There are those who challenge us. There will be in the future those who will challenge our doctrine, even challenge our Christianity. Love them and have the great confidence, the great peace within your own heart that you have a prophet, you have Apostles, you have light and knowledge of the purpose of life. Through revelation to prophets of God, you know who you are, where you came from, and why you are here; and you know your destiny as to where you will go in the world to come. May the Lord bless you, and may His peace be with you now and always.

These days that are before us are fraught with great sorrow and anguish and distress for the wicked among [us]; but following that night of darkness, of sorrow, of plague, of distress, of death and destruction, shall come the dawn, and the Redeemer shall come to live upon the earth and reign . . . for a thousand years; and we know it.

—MELVIN J. BALLARD

CHAPTER 11

THE ETERNAL PERSPECTIVE

I REMEMBER WELL the 2002 Winter Olympics that were hosted in Utah. It was a most remarkable time, one that we will never forget. We were able to attend a few of the events, including the opening ceremonies. I vividly recall the emotions as the flag that hung over the World Trade Center on September 11, 2001, was carried into the stadium. A quiet reverence fell over the stands as U.S. athletes and members of the New York police department carried in the flag that reminded us all of the tragedies of that day when terrorists attacked the United States. The Tabernacle Choir then performed the national anthem. That moment set a tone of gratitude and patriotism over the entire Olympic games.

In addition to the opening and closing ceremonies, we attended some of the ice-skating events and watched many other events from home. I was amazed at the years of preparation on the part of the athletes that led them to be qualified to participate in those games. I sometimes wonder how they stay upright on the ice, let alone do jumps and flips and land so gracefully. All of the athletes who participated were to be commended, and those great athletes who won the gold, silver, and bronze medals demonstrated commitment, sacrifice, and discipline that were remarkable to see. Their dedication to reach their goals through hard work and focused attention to details made them world champions.

I will now discuss what we must do to win the *eternal* gold that our Heavenly Father and the Lord Jesus Christ have prepared for the faithful followers of Christ. This prize excels any other accomplishment in life. The great thing about this contest is that each of us is in the competition, and every one of us can win the gold medal of eternal life.

To understand the goal of eternal life, we must understand the plan of salvation. In the Pearl of Great Price, we learn from Moses's account:

> And behold, the glory of the Lord was upon Moses, so that Moses stood in the presence of God, and talked with him face to face. And the Lord God said unto Moses: For mine own purpose have I made these things. Here is wisdom and it remaineth in me.
>
> And by the word of my power, have I created them, which is mine Only Begotten Son, who is full of grace and truth.
>
> And worlds without number have I created; and I also created them for mine own purpose; and by the Son I created them, which is mine Only Begotten.
>
> And the first man of all men have I called Adam, which is many.
>
> But only an account of this earth, and the inhabitants thereof, give I unto you. For behold, there are many worlds that have passed away by the word of my power. And there are many that now stand, and innumerable are they unto man; but all things are numbered unto me, for they are mine and I know them. (Moses 1:31–35)

When we contemplate the great power of the holy priesthood, we realize that God, our Eternal Heavenly Father, the Father of your spirit and the Father of mine, by and through the power of the holy priesthood, obtained His

> *God's love for [us] is manifest in many ways. The providing of this wonderful world, our existence in it, the comforts of life that come to us through His providing, are evidences of His love; but beyond all these and far greater is the gift of His beloved Son.*
>
> —Melvin J. Ballard

high standing and station in the eternal worlds. By and through the power of the holy priesthood, His Only Begotten was given the power and the capability to create this world. Jesus Christ was the firstborn spiritual son to our Father and our Mother in Heaven, and He is the Only Begotten Son of God our Eternal Heavenly Father in the flesh. He was given instructions to organize this earth. He was given instructions to separate the night from the day. He was given instructions to separate the land from the sea. He was given instructions to place life upon the earth, beginning with the animals. Then, ultimately, on the sixth day of creation, as we all know, that great moment came when God our Eternal Heavenly Father, in company with His Only Begotten Son, Jesus Christ, placed Adam and Eve upon the earth.

Be diligent and faithful in keeping inviolate the covenants you made in the waters of baptism. Ever strive to adhere strictly to the commandments of God, and with constant prayer and honest desire endeavor to overcome the weaknesses of human nature, and to conform your lives to the principles and doctrines of Christ upon which eternal life depends.
—Hyrum Mack Smith

And we reverence and we honor and we love our father Adam and mother Eve. Most people think of them as having committed a grievous sin, making them at least partly to blame for the difficulties that come into our lives. We declare instead that men and women "will be punished for their own sins, and not for Adam's transgression" (Articles of Faith 1:2). Unlike many others, we reverence Adam and Eve as our first earthly parents, and we honor our father Adam as prophet and Eve as "the mother of all living" (Moses 4:26).

We honor the Only Begotten Son, Jesus Christ, above all as the priesthood leader after whom we are to pattern our lives. It is significant that He said in His ministry as He walked among men, "Come, follow me" (Luke 18:22).

It was He who taught in the Sermon on the Mount that we

should be perfect even as our Father in Heaven is perfect (see Matthew 5:48). We are on a road through life trying to become just men and women "made perfect through Jesus the mediator of the new covenant, who wrought out this perfect atonement through the shedding of his own blood" (Doctrine and Covenants 76:69).

In that same great sermon, the Savior told the Saints who were gathered with Him on the mount, "Seek ye first the kingdom of God, and his righteousness; and all these things shall be added unto you" (Matthew 6:33). That is very significant instruction coming from the Savior of the world, to seek first the kingdom of God that all else might come unto us.

Now, I realize that it is difficult to always keep the eternal perspective. Sometimes we feel we are a long time separated from our Heavenly Father, a long way away. But when we have the eternal perspective in view, we recognize that earth life is really a very short period. I used to tell my missionaries in Canada as I tried to motivate them to work harder and be more dedicated, to sacrifice more completely in building the kingdom of God, that someday we will all look back and with perfect vision see life in its true, accurate perspective. I told them that in relationship to eternity, this earth life would be like taking an eyedropper, rowing out into the middle of Lake Ontario, and dropping one drop of water into that great body of water. And yet so much depends on what happens during this short segment of our eternal existence.

> *We are dual beings; we lived before we dwelt in the flesh—spiritual sons and daughters of our Father in Heaven, in whose presence we once dwelt and knew each other and knew Him.*
> —Melvin J. Ballard

I don't know how long we lived before we came here. I do know that we were born spiritually to our heavenly parents. I know that we lived with them for a considerable length of time before the decision was made by our Father in Heaven to create this earth through the labors of His Beloved Son.

Our Heavenly Father and the Savior of the world saw the end from the beginning. They were very much involved in our lives and in our training before we ever came here. They would like to be very much involved in your life and my life while we are here on this earth. They certainly want to be very much involved in our lives throughout all eternity.

God bless the Latter-day Saints, make them true and faithful. . . . Then I know that we shall arise again, to be exalted and to sit in glory in the celestial kingdom of our God, and praise be to God the Father and to Jesus Christ the Redeemer of the world, for this hope forever.
—Hyrum Mack Smith

As my wife and I raised seven children, it has been interesting to see that children seem to want to have everything their parents have. Sometimes when they get married and go off on their own, they like to start where their parents are, not realizing that it took their parents years of working together to get there. It is quite a shock to some of them to start in a little humble apartment with borrowed furniture and whatever Mother and Dad decide they can give to them. They would like to be like we are, and that's good; I think it is normal.

Similarly, you and I would like to be like our Father in Heaven. We would like to have what our Heavenly Father has for His sons and His daughters. What is promised to us as sons and daughters of God, our Eternal Heavenly Father? In what I believe is one of the greatest revelations that has ever been given, we read the following words about those who qualify for the celestial kingdom or the highest degree of glory that God has prepared for His children: "They are they into whose hands the Father has given all things" (Doctrine and Covenants 76:55).

It is difficult for me to fully comprehend what it means to have all that our Father in Heaven has.

Reading further: "Wherefore, as it is written, they are gods, even the sons of God—" (v. 58). Those who qualify for the highest degree of the celestial kingdom qualify for the highest of all priesthood callings, the calling to receive the powers and the abilities and the capabilities through the priesthood to officiate as a god.

The Lord continued: "These [those who qualify for the celestial kingdom] shall dwell in the presence of God and his Christ forever and ever" (v. 62). Here He made it clear to you and to me that our goal, our objective, and His desire for us as His children are to qualify to dwell in the presence of God and His Son forever and ever. "These are they whose bodies are celestial, whose glory is that of the sun, even the glory of God, the highest of all, whose glory the sun of the firmament is written of as being typical" (v. 70).

It is glorious and splendid in the terrestrial world, and even in the telestial world, where the glory of God will reign, for those are kingdoms of our Father, and His Son rules over them—but, great and splendid as they may be, still those who dwell there will feel remorse that they did not live worthy to obtain an inheritance upon the celestial world. How wonderful it is that our Father has given every one of us the privilege to be born here royal heirs.
—Melvin J. Ballard

Finally, when we read a few more verses in this great vision, we should start to realize the magnitude of the eternal perspective of life: "And thus we saw the glory of the celestial, which excels in all things—where God, even the Father, reigns upon his throne forever and ever; before whose throne all things bow in humble reverence, and give him glory forever and ever. They who dwell in his presence are the church of the Firstborn; and they see as they are seen, and know as they are known, having received of his fulness and of his grace; and he makes them equal in power, and in might, and in dominion. And the glory of the celestial is one, even as the glory of the sun is one" (Doctrine and Covenants 76:92–96).

If we live worthily, if we keep the commandments, if we repent of our sins, if we believe in Jesus Christ, if we seek to become perfect in Christ, if we seek first the kingdom of God, if we can learn to set earthly pleasure and mortality in second place and give primary attention to the eternal perspective, the day will come when all that our Father has to give to His children will be shared by Him.

> *I have no words to speak against the accumulation of this world's goods. I have discovered, however, from the experiences of men who have been successful in this line, that money does not bring happiness, and that it often happens that when they have amassed a fortune, there is always something else they would rather have than the money they have accumulated. Those who have succeeded in winning the plaudits of the world, through the development of their talents, have often longed for something else that they would rather have.*
>
> —Melvin J. Ballard

I had an interesting experience some years ago that helped me learn how important it is in life to keep an eternal perspective. I was in business with Art Linkletter and many other major entertainers in the United States. We built a theatre in North Salt Lake called the Valley Music Hall. Through that experience, I met many of the great stars when they came to perform and entertain there. I became a very close and dear friend of Art Linkletter. We were involved in another project that required substantial financing. He thought he knew just the man who might be interested in financing this project, so arrangements were made to have him take a look at it.

I was invited to fly to Los Angeles, where I boarded a corporate jet. We then flew to Mexico to look at the project Mr. Linkletter and I were interested in. On board the jet was a multibillionaire who was one of the ten wealthiest men on the earth at that time. Also seated in very luxurious chairs were a multimillionaire; Art Linkletter, another multimillionaire; and me. As we flew toward Mazatlan, Mexico, I listened to the discussion that went on among these three wealthy business magnates as it related to earthly holdings and worldly goods. They talked about purchasing multimillion-dollar organizations.

Finally, there was a lull in the conversation, and the billionaire asked me, "What do you do, Mr. Ballard?" I thought carefully how to answer the question, knowing I was struggling to make ends meet. I finally said, "I have a wonderful wife, seven great children, a comfortable home, and good friends like Art Linkletter." There was a pause. I then asked the billionaire, "How many children do you have?" His answer was, "I do not have any children."

Then Art Linkletter did exactly what I hoped someone would do. He said, "My friend, what are you going to do with all of your money?" The reply: "Well, I'm going to give it to charity and a lot of it to the cancer society for research." Then Art, with his great sense of humor, said, "Why don't you give some of it now?" The billionaire replied, "I'm not going to give any of it now; I'll control it all until I die and then they can do what they want to with it." Art then said, "I'd give some of it to the cancer society now. You might get cancer, and with your gift, they might find a cure and keep you alive." His friend didn't think that was funny at all.

Thank God, men and women . . . who are full of the principles of the gospel of Jesus Christ and the love of the truth, are willing to do their duty and fulfill the measure of their creation, to become fathers and mothers in Israel, with the hope and knowledge that in thus obeying God they are laying the foundations for their kingdoms and exaltations, in the presence of the eternal Father.

—Hyrum Mack Smith

Then, as we started talking about things of real meaning in life, I began to think that this man with his billions of dollars was miserable. He had only one thing on his mind—and that was making more and more money. When I arrived home from that trip, I walked into the house and Barbara greeted me. She said, "Well, how did things go?" And my answer was, "Sweetheart, I learned one thing: of the four men who were on that plane, I was by far the wealthiest. I was the only one on board who knew where I came from, why I was here, and where I could go if I was willing to pay the price."

The day will come when that billionaire will die, and he will not take one penny with him. He will not take any of his earthly belongings. He will not take any of his homes. All the riches he has will stay here. When I die, because I am willing to try to keep the commandments and continue repenting of my sins with "unshaken faith" in Christ, "relying wholly upon the merits of him who is mighty to save" (2 Nephi 31:19), I will take my wealth with me—my testimony, what I have come to know to be true, and the eternal relationships I have made in this life with my wife, my children, and my friends.

> *A soul redeemed and sanctified and worthy to enter into the highest degree of celestial glory is of greater intrinsic worth than all the wealth of all the world.*
> —Melvin J. Ballard

I hope I can walk with head held high into the presence of God the Eternal Father and His Beloved Son, the Savior and Redeemer of the world, and feel comfortable and welcome to come into Their presence and spend the eternities with Them.

I suggest to you that when we keep the eternal perspective in view, it doesn't matter where we live. It doesn't matter what we own. It doesn't matter how many earthly belongings we have. The only thing that really matters is the kind of a person I have become. What kind of perspective do I have? What kind of real interest do I have in others? The things you remember the most are the things you have done for other people and never the things you do for yourself.

I think of a dear sister who lived in our ward when I was about twelve years old. Her husband died suddenly of a heart attack, and

I remember I had the impression that I ought to do something nice for her. I didn't know what I could do, but I went to her home to visit her because her husband had been the secretary in the Aaronic Priesthood program, and we all loved him. As I walked onto her front porch, I noticed that the paint was all chipped and peeling off. I had the impression that somebody ought to paint the porch for her. I went back to my father and said, "Will you buy the paint if I paint the porch?" He was glad to do it. I went down and painted her porch.

That woman suffered problems in life that are just unbelievable. Shortly after the loss of her husband, one of her sons-in-law took his own life. Then another son-in-law had a serious accident that almost took his life. She sent her only son on a full-time mission, and he contracted polio and came home to her paralyzed from the neck down. She faced problem after problem, but she was always happy. Whenever we went to her home, she greeted us fondly. She never forgot that I had painted her porch, and I never forgot what a great pleasure that was for me.

Live together in love and affectionate fellowship as becometh disciples of the Lord, supporting and defending one another in all righteousness, and bearing with patience and the spirit of forgiveness each other's infirmities.

—Hyrum Mack Smith

This dear sister lived by the eternal perspective. A lot of people came to her and said, "How do you stand all these difficulties and problems that have been dealt to you?" Some were even critical of the Lord for allowing all these problems to come to one individual. She had the power and the strength to think and to live eternally. I suppose she was given those kinds of trials because she could bear them and thereby set an example for many of her brothers and sisters on the earth who thought they had troubles until they saw what real trouble was and what she had been through. She lived a great life. When she passed away, the chapel was filled for her funeral. Everybody loved this dear sister who lived by the eternal perspective.

The thing I remember most about this sister was that little deed I did for her just because I felt it was something I ought to do. I submit to you that as you look back on your life, you will think about the time you visited the widow or the time you helped the orphan or the time you helped the unfortunate or took a loaf of bread to the neighbors. Those are the things that have eternal meaning. Do you remember the last movie you went to or the score of the last ballgame you attended? Those memories fade quickly, but you never forget the things you do for other people. They stay with you; they are eternal.

> *Not until the kingdom of God is found within us as well as outside of us, can we hope for peace on earth and good will for men.*
> —Hyrum Mack Smith

Do you remember the lawyer who tried to challenge the Savior? He came to Jesus and asked which of all the commandments was the most important. The Savior didn't hesitate; He responded quickly and positively: "Thou shalt love the Lord thy God with all thy heart, and with all thy soul, and with all thy mind." And then He went on a step further and said, "And the second is like unto it, Thou shalt love thy neighbour as thyself" (Matthew 22:36–39).

Those are the first two great commandments as spoken by the Savior of the world. When you and I learn to keep the eternal perspective in view—when we really love the Lord our God with all our heart, might, mind, and strength—we never compromise what we know to be true. We hang in there regardless of how tough things get, and we hold tight to the things we believe to be true.

When the Savior of this world came to the earth, one of His main purposes was to break the bonds of death and to make it possible for all the sons and daughters of God our Heavenly Father to go back into His presence and live eternally. That possibility would become a reality only upon a resurrection from the dead. Up to the time of the coming of the Only Begotten Son of God into this world to live and die here, there was no resurrection. I cannot comprehend His suffering in the Garden of Gethsemane as He took upon Himself the sins of this world. The scriptures record that tragic time in His life as He carried His own cross and fell from exhaustion after being beaten and spat upon and abused. The cross was lifted off of Him and put on someone else to carry the balance of the way to Calvary. On that cross, the Son of God gave His life for you and for me.

In His three-year ministry, Jesus Christ laid out very clearly and precisely what you and I have to do to inherit the blessings mentioned earlier in those passages from the Doctrine and Covenants. If we want to dwell in the presence of God our Eternal Heavenly Father and His Son, Jesus Christ, throughout all eternity, we have to live the gospel and keep the commandments on the Savior's terms, and not on ours. Those terms are made abundantly clear in His teachings.

> *How is the battle going with you? How is it going with men and women in the world? That is a very important question. The greatest conflict that any man or woman will ever have, I care not how numerous their enemies may be, will be the battle that is had with self.*
>
> —Melvin J. Ballard

The Savior of the world has led the way. He has established His Church. He has given us the plan. We are not trying to build our lives like a builder might try to build a building without an architectural plan. We have the plan called the gospel of Jesus Christ.

When we understand the gospel of Jesus Christ and really have it in perspective, then we think eternally. We will never question the need for a Savior. We will never question the Father's love in sending His Son into the world to save us. We won't wonder about keeping the covenants or the commandments when we think eternally. Specifically, we will never question the law of tithing; we won't argue about the Word of Wisdom. We won't question the need to come to priesthood or

Relief Society meetings or to sacrament meeting or Sunday School. We realize the importance of being humble followers of Christ. We accept the invitation from our loving Heavenly Father to love God and to love all men and women.

> *The ground is being leveled for the palace of the King, the New Jerusalem. Old institutions are giving way to the new that will take their place. And when our Father and our God has finished His work of redemption of this earth, we shall sing His praise and shout for joy, as we did when the foundations of this same earth were laid in the morning of creation.*
> —Hyrum Mack Smith

We want to do those things necessary to go and dwell in the presence of God and Jesus Christ throughout all eternity. Through faith in Jesus Christ, repentance, baptism, the gift of the Holy Ghost, and enduring to the end, it all can be ours if we think straight.

I bear witness to you that the Savior lives. He is the Beloved Son of God. He is the Only Begotten. He is Jehovah of the Old Testament. He is the promised Messiah (Christ) of the New Testament. He is the Resurrected Lord. He is the God of Israel and the God of the whole earth. He is the Redeemer of this world. He is our Advocate with the Father. He will come again and reign as the King of kings and Lord of lords.

Through Jesus Christ, we have a promise of life eternal. Without Him, life is empty and shallow, without eternal meaning and perspective. With the Son of God as our friend, as our Savior and Redeemer, life then takes on eternal perspective.

Please remember life on this earth is but a moment. Let us not waste any time. Let us be anxiously engaged. Let us be dedicated, striving with all our hearts to seek first the kingdom of God. Let us go for the *real* gold.

Sources

Ballard, M. Russell. *Counseling with Our Councils.* 2012.

———. *Our Search for Happiness.* 1993.

Benson, Ezra Taft. "'Come unto Christ, and Be Perfected in Him.'" *Ensign,* May 1988.

Cline, Victor B. "Handcart Pioneers Through the Ages." *Instructor,* February 1967.

Daughters in My Kingdom: The History and Work of Relief Society. 2011.

Guide to the Scriptures. Available online at www.lds.org/scriptures /gs?lang=eng.

Hinckley, Gordon B. "Living in the Fulness of Times." *Ensign,* November 2001, 5–6.

———. "The Times in Which We Live." *Ensign,* November 2001, 74.

Hymns of The Church of Jesus Christ of Latter-day Saints. 1985.

"Hyrum Mack Smith." *Improvement Era*, March 1918.

Journal of Discourses. 26 vols. 1854–1886.

Kimball, Spencer W. *Faith Precedes the Miracle.* 1972.

———. *My Beloved Sisters.* 1979.

Lectures on Faith. 1985.

Madsen, Truman G. *The Highest in Us.* 1978.

Masterpieces of Religious Verse. Edited by James Dalton Morrison. 1948.

Maxwell, Neal A. "'Deny Yourselves of All Ungodliness.'" *Ensign,* May 1995.

McKay, David O. "The Atonement." *Instructor,* March 1959.

Nelson, Russell M. "Lessons from Eve." *Ensign,* November 1987.

Packer, Boyd K. "Reverence Invites Revelation." *Ensign,* November 1991.

Preach My Gospel. 2005.

Random House Dictionary of the English Language. 2nd ed. 2005.

Smith, Joseph. *History of the Church of Jesus Christ of Latter-day Saints.* 7 vols. 1932–1951.

———. *Teachings of the Prophet Joseph Smith.* Selected and arranged by Joseph Fielding Smith. 1976.

Smith, Joseph F. *Gospel Doctrine: Selections from the Sermons and Writings of Joseph F. Smith.* 1939.

Snow, Eliza R. "Great Indignation Meeting." *The Deseret Evening News,* January 14, 1870.

Talmage, James E. *Jesus the Christ.* 1982.

"The Family: A Proclamation to the World." *Ensign*, November 2010.

Woodruff, Wilford. "Discourse Delivered at the Weber Stake Conference, Ogden, Monday, October 19th, 1896, by Prest. Wilford Woodruff," *The Deseret Weekly,* vol. 53, no. 21 (November 7, 1896), 642–43.

INDEX